GETTING NAKED

GETTING NAKED

The Bare Necessities
of Entrepreneurship and Start Ups

By Joel Primus
with
Bennett R. Coles

Cover Design by: Jackie Friesen
Cover Photo Taken by Derek Atchison, 2015
Two years before sale of Naked

Interior Design by: Mariana Coello

ISBNs:
978-1-77374-074-4 (Paperback)
978-1-77374-075-1 (Hardcover)
978-1-77374-076-8 (eBook)
978-1-77374-077-5 (Audiobook)

DEKAN Publishing
Vancouver, BC, Canada

Dedication

To all those entrepreneurs out there …
Take it one step at a time and don't stop believing
in yourself!

Acknowledgments

To my co-author Ben Coles, who patiently worked beside me on this project for nearly eight years!

To my family, for believing in me as I chased yet another goal.

To my incredible business partners along the way: Alex McAulay, Karyna McLaren, Travis McLaren, Ross Brown, Andrew Kaplan, Carole & David Hochman, and Phil Gurat.

To Joanne Maurits for your creativity, passion, and support for this story.

And to all those incredible people who made the time to help an entrepreneur on his journey.

Table of contents

Introduction

If you're an entrepreneur dreaming of building an incredibly successful business, the cold, harsh truth is that you have a 90% chance of failing. [1]

Like you, I'm sure, my own optimism and confidence led me to believe that I'd end up on the "one out of ten" side that breaks through to the rarified air of a ridiculously successful sale of my first business.

I was mostly wrong. Moreover, I never expected my journey as an entrepreneur to be so full of personal sacrifices and hardships, isolation, anxiety, and challenges on the road to becoming the person I wanted to be.

But why do 90% of startups fail? And why would the well-being of your personal life and mental health be so inextricably tied to the success of a company?

Well, the first mistake people make when starting companies is that they fail to realize that, as Ed Zschau says, "Entrepreneurship is an approach to life." It's not just a game of monopoly.

One of the goals of a startup is to no longer be a startup, yet one of the biggest reasons nine out of ten startups fail is scaling (growing) too fast.

As Colin R Davis once said, "The road to success and the road to failure are almost exactly the same."

---

[1] UC Berkeley. Marmer, M., Herrmann, B.J., Dogrultan, E., & Berman, R. (2011, August 29). Startup Genome. [web log post] Startup Genome Report Extra on Premature Scaling. Retrieved from: https://innovationfootprints.com/wp-content/uploads/2015/07/startup-genome-report-extra-on-premature-scaling.pdf

What Mr. Davis's quote means, I've come to learn, is that the roads to success and failure are the exact same—it's the same road. Only that the road to success is a hell of a lot longer and it's paved with our failures along the way.

Getting Naked is a book about those failures. It's about the misses, missteps, misunderstandings, mishaps and mis-directions that lead us exactly where we actually need to go. It's a book about the important details that often lay hidden in the balance of starting our first business venture. The first part of the book asks a lot of questions and focuses on real experiences, to get you thinking like an entrepreneur. The second part of the book is more instructional, with some basic principles I think every business person should know. The final part of the book is experiential again, with some concluding questions that are worth thinking about as you consider the long game.

We're going to start with questions as simple as *how do we recognize what business we should start and what does it feel like to take the leap to start it?* For a taste of that, let's start with a little story I once read about salt.

Salt? Yes, salt.

"Once upon a time there was a rich merchant with a fleet of ships and three sons, the youngest of whom was small in stature. One spring, the merchant gave his older sons ships laden with furs, carpets and fine linens, instructing one to sail east and one to sail west in search of new kingdoms with which to trade. When the youngest son asked where his boat was, the merchant and the older boys laughed. In the end, the merchant gave his youngest son a rickety sloop with raggedy sails, a toothless crew and empty sacks for ballast. When the young man asked his father in which direction he should sail, the merchant replied that he should sail until the sun never sets in December.

So the son sailed southward with his scurvy crew. After months on the open seas they reached a land where the sun never set in

December. There, they landed on an island that appeared to have a mountain of snow, but which turned out to be a mountain of salt. Salt was so plentiful in his homeland that the housewives cast it over their shoulders for good luck without a second thought. Nonetheless, the young man instructed his crew to fill the sacks in the hull with the salt, if for no other reason than to add to the ship's ballast.

Sailing truer and faster than before, they soon came upon a great kingdom. The king received the merchant's son in his court and asked what he had to trade. The young man replied that he had a hull full of salt. Remarking that he had never heard of it, the king wished him well and sent him back on his way. Undaunted, the young man paid a visit to the king's kitchens, where he discreetly sprinkled salt onto the mutton, into the soup, over the tomatoes, and into the custard.

That night, the king was amazed at the flavor of his food. The mutton was better, the soup was better, the tomatoes were better, even the custard was better. Calling his chefs before him, he excitedly asked what new technique they were using. Befuddled, the chefs admitted they had done nothing different; although they had been visited in the kitchen by the young stranger from the sea …

The next afternoon, the merchant's son set sail for home in a ship laden with one bag of gold for every sack of salt." [2]

This young man's journey is no different than your journey as an entrepreneur. The story entails setting out on your own path, leading a team and finding an opportunity in a product and delivering it to a "market" that actually wants it … even if it take a few tries for them to realize they do!

What our little salt story downplays is the reality that this savvy, determined young son of a rich merchant was also a fool. At least in the beginning! And on his epic journey he was, as Jordan Peterson puts it, a "transforming fool."

2 Towles, A. (2016). A Gentleman in Moscow. New York. Penguin Random House

So what does that mean?

Well, we all don't know what we don't know, so when we set out to discover and try new things, we're sometimes going to be foolish. This foolishness isn't bad, though: it's a rite of passage. Approaching things for the first time may result in foolish actions and most new ideas may seem foolish in and of themselves—at least to others. Haven't your ideas been called foolish before? I know mine certainly have.

But you have to be a fool before you can be a master. And if you're not willing to be a bit of a fool … you're never going to reach the unknown heights you are striving for!

Besides, if you want to do something, like start a business, I tend to think that it's better to do something a bit foolishly than not at all. Of course, I'm not promising mastery here either, that's for you to discover as you go. If, however, I can point you in the right direction to limit some of that foolishness then I've done what I hoped to do with this book.

You can be a fool once, maybe even twice. But as you move through life you'll uncover that experiences (lessons) will keep repeating themselves until you've actually learned them. In a business, this gets expensive and can lead to failure. Throughout the book I'll share a few of my own run-ins with epic foolishness!

As an entrepreneur I started a bootcamp, a magazine, and then I started an underwear company called Naked. All more or less failed … at least in my opinion. All of them also had major silver linings that paved the way for incredible successes, relationships, and experiences that I wouldn't trade for anything.

For example, take this book you're just starting to read. My co-author Ben Coles was my boss at a newspaper company I used to work for. How did I get the job there? Well, I tried to sell them the magazine I'd started and instead they gave me a job selling ads and a consistent pay cheque (the last one I've ever had). Ben not only became a good friend, but he became the largest shareholder in my first investment round at Naked. When did he decide to invest, you ask? Well, no sooner than the week after he had to fire me from the newspaper!

Crazy, I know, but that's how this all works ... When we pause, pull back, and take a look at the events of our lives, we'll see that failures, heartbreak, and hardship can flow into opportunities, joy, and success—they all connect. It's when we're "in it" that we find these beautiful connections so hard to see, yet it's when we're in it that it matters most that we see them. For seeing them allows us to remain present in the moment, so we can still enjoy the life we're living and the presence of the people we're living it with; seeing these connections helps us remain calm under pressure so our teams can also remain calm and focused on the end result.

I've filled this book with many of those lessons and experiences, as well as ideas and tips for specific tasks like: starting a business; raising money; building a company and a brand; having shareholders; and dealing with clients, business partners, failure, and radical change. We'll dive into understanding what's essential and what's not in both your business and your life, as well as how to be a great (at least decent) business partner, spouse, and human being on planet Earth.

We'll explore this all by travelling through the startup journey of my first company Naked. I've read hundreds of amazing books but most were written so many years after the author's experiences that I felt they were out of touch with the realities of being in an entrepreneurial start up. That is why I started writing this book (more as a journal initially) the day I started Naked—I wanted to write the book I wish I could have read when I was starting my first company.

Ultimately though, this is your adventure. This is your own "hero's journey"—you've picked up this book because entrepreneurship is your chosen path on that journey. The "gold" you're looking for— be it fame, success, money, creditability, fulfillment—will be found deep down in a dark lair guarded by a fire breathing monster. That's not just where you'll *have* to go, but where you *should* go, to find it! That's how you become the person you're meant to be.

I've kept this book as short as I can for a reason. You have work to do and more books to read. My objective is purely to get you "thinking" about the myriad things you need to know or may encounter on your start up. For topics where I haven't provided a great deal of information in the narrative, there's an appendix of books I recommend for diving deeper into a subject.

Lastly, while I can assure you that everything in this story certainly happened, I've taken some narrative liberties with respect to the identities of the people who were involved. I've also changed some of the names, job titles, locations or timing of events. That said, let's get started on the journey.

1

Recognize Your Vision

Running away from Peruvian pimps isn't the safest way to start your business. I don't recommend it.

But it's how I started down the path to creating Naked Boxer Briefs, and it does support one of my core beliefs for young entrepreneurs: get out into that big, messy, old world and experience new things—a different perspective can bring clarity of vision.

Do you have a vision for what you want to accomplish? If so, where did it come from? If not, how can you develop a vision? Starting a business is a huge undertaking, and if you want any chance of success you need to have a clear, developed, and inspiring vision before you even start. As my own story shows, this isn't easy or linear, but the adventures along the way make it all worthwhile.

Experience Life First

For me, my business vision started on a hot, steamy night in Lima, Peru. My brother O'Neil and I, 18 years old and 21, respectively, had set out from our home near Vancouver to create a world-wide documentary film we called Project World Citizen. We'd already crossed more than a thousand kilometers of Central and South America, and had just that day dropped a thousand dollars to get our second video camera out of the customs lock-up. We'd begrudgingly forked over the extortion cash in order to keep our dream going. We were tired, bickering almost constantly, and our friend had just told us he was bailing on the project and not flying down to join us.

Suffice to say, things were not going well.

But that evening, with our equipment secure in the youth hostel locker, we joined the local owner of the hostel at a nearby club.

Now let me explain right from the start that the hostel owner, Alessandra, had my full attention. She was a few years older than me, and moved and spoke with that exotic, Latin style that could melt a skinny white guy like me. Dark, depthless eyes fixed on me with a casual sultriness that might have been an invitation, or might have been just an unconscious manifestation of innate sensuality. Either way, this had never happened to me before and I was hooked.

Some of the other travelers in the hostel had suggested we all check out this club, and as soon as I knew Alessandra was going, I changed into my last set of clean clothes and took my place at her side.

The club was crowded, low-ceilinged and dimly-lit. A haze of smoke obscured the mass of people huddled around tables drinking and watching the throbbing mass of the dance floor.

Alessandra leaned in to shout in my ear. "What do you think?"

"This place is awesome!" I exclaimed.

As she pulled back, her expression was lit up in surprise. I smiled at her—maybe she thought I'd never been to a serious club before. This place was exactly what I imagined a Latin nightclub to be. She gave me another long look with those dark, liquid eyes, then turned to follow O'Neil and the other girls from the hostel.

There was the obligatory standing around the rail at the edge of the dance floor while O'Neil bought several rounds of shots for everyone and I winced at the thought of our dwindling bank account. I could feel Alessandra swaying to the beat next to me. Reading the signs was not a skill I had particular aptitude for so I just savored my cerveza while O'Neil focused on another round of shots. I'd always found talking next to impossible in night clubs, which was a relief since I lost all confidence around beautiful women and could rarely string a coherent sentence together, let alone say anything witty.

Two or three shots later, everyone seemed ready to dance, and O'Neil led the charge. I took Alessandra's hand and led her out, following the now buzzed group into the undulating mass of bodies. I carved out a spot and faced her, surprised at how much the other women on the floor were obviously eyeing me up. Even better, Alessandra pressed in close, dancing in that Latin style which made sweat sexy.

Bodies gyrated to the rhythmic pumping of the beat, and all around us couples were starting to openly make out on the dance floor. Alessandra obviously noticed, too, and she kept her eyes locked on mine. I leaned in to kiss her.

She pulled back, shaking her head with a slight smile, even as she continued to dance.

Some girls from our hostel suddenly emerged from the throng, both flushed and glistening. Neither looked happy. Alessandra broke free to speak to them, but I couldn't hear their words over the pounding music and, I noticed suddenly, O'Neil was nowhere to be seen. I tapped Alessandra's shoulder.

"Where's O'Neil?" I shouted in her ear.

She motioned for me to wait, still speaking to her friends. A few more words were exchanged, then the other girls headed off the dance floor.

Alessandra turned to me. "Come with me."

I followed willingly, if still slightly confused. We reached the first of the tables beyond the dance floor, and Alessandra took a seat. The other girls kept walking, slipping through the crowd and headed for the door. I sat down.

"Where are they going? And where's O'Neil?"

Alessandra motioned toward a nearby table. I followed her gaze and spotted my brother, deep in a passionate lip-lock with some local girl. Apparently, the kid had figured out something I hadn't. All around them, men and women laughed and chatted. Other men sat silently in the shadows, watching stoically like they owned the joint.

The dancing had long since perspired out any feeling of the alcohol in my system, and I suddenly frowned as I realized something: despite all his teenage swagger, O'Neil wasn't exactly the most suave or charismatic man in the world. Women didn't just throw themselves at him, and my Spidey sense started to sound the alarm bells. I cast my eyes across the smoky club again—at all the other amorous couples entwined around us. Some couples were even now headed toward the doors. I turned to Alessandra, a cold pit of fear growing in my gut.

"What kind of club is this?"

She stared at me in amazement. "You don't know?"

"I'm starting to get an idea!"

Her dark eyes assessed me carefully, and I saw shades of wonder, humor, and even pity flash through them.

"Are you telling me," I said, "that most of the girls in here are working?"

She nodded her head.

"Did you know that when we came in?"

"No, I've never been here—it's a place the foreigners go. But I figured it out pretty fast. Why do you think I stuck so close to you? I don't want any foreign perverts trying to buy me."

My enthusiasm for the whole evening was starting to fade pretty damn quick. Time to go home.

"You better get your brother out of here," she said.

"No kidding."

She pulled me to my feet. "No, I mean you better get him out of here before he gets killed."

I stared at her.

She sighed, her disapproval clear. "The girls told me that this is the third one he's … engaged with. He settles in with one girl for a bit, then takes off into the crowd, then sits down with another."

I was already moving through the tables, noticing that the silent men in the shadows were all watching O'Neil. And me.

Alessandra grabbed my arm. "Stand back. Let me break them up and you get him out of here."

I paused while she strode past me, marching right up to O'Neil and grabbing his face at the cheeks. She shouted at him in rapid-fire Spanish, gesturing wildly. The girl leaned back slightly, glaring at this newcomer but not interfering. O'Neil stared up at Alessandra with a stunned, drunken gaze.
Alessandra turned and motioned me over, still shouting in Spanish. I took her cue and approached, taking my brother by the arm and pulling him up. O'Neil fought me off.

I leaned in to hiss in his ear. "These are all *prostitutes*, and you aren't paying. See those guys over there in the shadows … they're the ones who'll be collecting if we don't get the hell out of here!"

O'Neil stared at me strangely, but didn't resist as I hauled him to his feet and hustled him toward the door. Alessandra was right behind us, still shouting wildly. No-one blocked our passage. Even the two gun-toting guards let us pass, dim amusement in their eyes.

Outside on the street, the Lima air was cool and soft, and as Alessandra' s stream of cursing finally faded out, I released my brother and turned to her.

"What was all that?" I asked.

She shook her head. "I pretended O'Neil was my boyfriend, and that I was furious at him. I don't know if anyone believed me, but it worked."

O'Neil was still stunned, eyes darting between us.

"Thanks. I think you saved our asses." I gave her my best smile, trying to act like I was completely chill in situations like this. The reality was my heart was still pounding. "Let's get back to the hostel."

"No way," she said, taking both our hands and leading us in the opposite direction. "Somebody might decide to follow us, and I'm not leading them back to my place."

I pulled her to a stop. "Whoa. Then where *are* we going?"

"Somewhere with lots of people."

Barely two blocks away, the dim streets opened up into a somewhat-less-dim square. Most of the illumination came from the spotlights on the white-washed tower of the church, but around the edges of the square stood lamps in front of ramshackle stalls. It must have been midnight, but the stalls were all open and a respectable crowd of shoppers mingled about.

Following Alessandra, I blended in with the light crowd moving along in front of the stands. It was a real mix of products for sale. A couple of stalls had the usual tourist shit on offer, but most of the entrepreneurs seemed to be interested in the local traffic. There was farm produce, phone cards, CDs and DVDs, gadgets and minor appliances, key-cutters, and even chickens and other water birds. Every stall seemed to have a portable generator to provide light and power, and for a temporary market I was pretty impressed.

I paused at a stall selling clothes. The nights here brought sweet relief from the daytime temperatures, but the humidity still clung like a wool blanket. Although laundry was cheap on the road, we were sweating like pigs and I'd worn out a few pairs of underwear. A few extra pairs of cheap underwear would be, I thought, a good investment.

Conscious of Alessandra beside me, I wondered what she'd think about my underwear shopping on a date … was it a date at this point? I peered past the bored shopkeeper toward his wares. Spotting some boxer briefs, I stepped into the stall and grabbed the first pair.

As soon as the fabric slid between my hands, I started to pay more attention. This was something different. It was smooth like silk, but stretchy. Soft like cotton, but light. I held up the pair to examine the design. Almost seamless. A small, thin waistband. Curious, I checked the label: nothing I'd ever heard of before.

I stood there, knowing that Alessandra was watching me as I stared at bags of underwear but unable to tear my eyes away.

Alessandra touched my arm. "I think it's fine to head home, now. Do you have what you need?"

"Yeah," I said, grabbing five packages of the boxer briefs. "I think I do."

I'd like to say that, from the moment I picked up those boxers in a Peruvian night market while I hid out from pimps, the future became clear and I moved from one inevitable step to the next on my way to success. But real life is a lot messier than that. For one thing, at the time I thought my vision was to create an award-winning documentary which would propel me to Hollywood glory—the underwear was just a necessity in equatorial climes.

But as Project World Citizen slowly crashed down like the train wreck it was becoming, as O'Neil and I continued to argue over the merits of the project, as I postured for the camera and he over-directed me, as our savings dwindled away, and as our best camera—the one we'd paid a thousand dollars to liberate from Peruvian customs—tumbled down the rocky cliffs in the Atacama desert of Chile to its destruction, as our entire vision collapsed, I kept thinking about those amazing boxer briefs I'd bought. Two pairs never even left the plastic bags I bought them in, even as I lugged them around South America in my backpack.

When O'Neil and I finally returned home to Canada, exhausted, broke, and with no movie to speak of, I strangely wasn't depressed. I was disappointed that we hadn't achieved what we set out to do, but the experience had given me a rich, new perspective on the world. I already had a new vision forming, and I knew my road ahead was in a different direction.

Your Thoughts Create Your Reality

I set out on my South American adventure with a goal in mind, and even though things didn't work out the way I expected, I was always open to possibilities. My dream of making a film didn't die on that trip—it just got pushed back as I realized how little I knew about film-making. But even as that idea faded into the background, a new vision started to form, centered on those amazing boxers. I didn't know what that vision was, not yet, but I knew it was worth focusing on.

Once you have a vision in your mind, keep thinking about it. You might not be in a position to act on it right away, but the more you mull it over the more vivid the vision can become. Do research on the topic, talk to people who are already in that field, and learn as much as you can about what you want to do—before you actually commit to doing it.

You might discover, for example, that there are professional or educational requirements that you must have before you can even enter the field. Or you might, in your research, realize that what you thought was an original idea has already been done a dozen times. These might seem like roadblocks, but really they're new, relevant bits of information that you can bring into your thought process and vision. If you need to earn a professional qualification first, you can now start to visualize how you'll accomplish that necessary first step. If you find that your "original" idea isn't new, you can study what others have done and develop another, more advanced, differentiated or relevant idea that truly is unique. The key is to keep learning, and to keep experiencing life while thinking about your vision.

Your thoughts create your reality. They shape how you see the world, how you approach every challenge and every opportunity. We're all thinking creatures. The more aware you are of your thoughts, and the more you direct them, the more focused you can be.

Often we latch onto something that we're really good at. Makes sense, because if you're going to build your career on something, it helps to begin with a natural advantage. So start there, and see if you can build a vision on your strengths. Be careful, though, because assessing your own strengths can be difficult if you don't have much to compare them to. Be careful also that you don't put your strengths on too high a pedestal.

The mental story I'd always told myself as a teenager seemed to go like this: "I'm good at _____ (fill in the blank), therefore, I should like and do _____ in order to have purpose, to be successful and to craft an identity."

Running was the first thing I was ever good at. I was a track star in high school (which, by the way, is very, very different from being a football star), was a provincial champion, a national cross country team member, represented Canada at the World Youth Games and had earned a full scholarship to the University of High Point in North Carolina. Running was my life, and as a teenager I could see no other path toward success.

If you're like me, your idea puts you on a path. A path that, once you're on, can be hard to step away from unless SNAP—something goes wrong and that path isn't viable anymore. In my case, it was a literal snap of my Achilles tendon that ended my running career in my first year of university. Your snap might be metaphorical, but as your path shatters in a million places and you can't do the thing you were supposed to do for the rest of your life, you can find yourself lost.

Remember, your thoughts create your reality. When trouble comes your way, avoid the real temptation to despair. The sudden end of a path isn't the end of your existence—it's just the end of that path. Look around. There are other paths. Some might branch directly off the path you were following, and others might require a big leap to reach. But there's always a path forward, and the old path you left behind just becomes part of your broader experience of life.

When you face the world with openness and curiosity, ready to cast aside old beliefs and habits, ready for whatever you might discover, your experiences offer you many ideas, rich with purpose and passion. They may never have come to you if you'd hadn't taken that first, bold step. Being spontaneous will add another splash of magic to your experiences. There's less fear of failure and fewer expectations when you're spontaneous. But being spontaneous requires letting go and surrendering to whatever appears, which can be hard if you're a person who likes to have a plan. All I can say is that the excitement that ensues from spontaneity can fill you up with such a zest for life that you feel unstoppable.

When I couldn't be an elite runner anymore, I admit that I wallowed in despair for a while. I couldn't see any other path, mostly because

I'd been wearing "running blinders" for so many years that I couldn't recognize any other paths. Being a runner was my identity—and a runner who can't run is nothing. My advice to you here is simple: you are much more than just one thing. You might have a primary aspect of your life with which you most identify, but if that aspect gets taken away from you, don't despair—there's a lot more of you in there just waiting to shine.

When my running dreams were lying shattered at my feet, I decided to travel. First, I hitch-hiked across Canada, then I did a bit of world travel. The hitch-hiking was dirt-cheap (sleeping in the open prairie in a tent is both humbling and inspiring) and I'd worked enough bartending jobs to save some money to travel overseas. Six months on the beach in Thailand was a huge departure for this small-town boy, and while I can't say that on my first trip abroad I had any huge epiphanies about what to do with my life, I certainly came home with a broader perspective and a belief that the world was bursting with opportunities. I was finally able to see past my running career, and cast around for a new vision for myself. My next vision was to keep travelling, but to film a documentary as I went. This didn't work out right away like I'd hoped, but it gave me my first hard experience in dealing with budgets and business partners, and it did take me to a certain Peruvian night market.

Your thoughts create your reality, as your mind directs your choices toward supporting your vision whenever it can. If you focus on your vision, you'll be amazed at the people and opportunities you uncover that can help you.

I went through a multi-year exploration, following ideas and new opportunities as they arose, and gathering experiences along the way. I was eventually led to start an underwear company called Naked. If you'd told me after my first year of university—that 19-year-old, proud, virgin-runner-geek who wore hand-me-down clothing—that in three years I'd be running a company in the high-fashion underwear business, I'd have laughed at you. At 19 I didn't know what I didn't know, (obviously) but my parents had instilled in me that essential ability to look beyond my immediate situation, to dream big, and to create vision.

You might be considering your path right now. You might have an idea that you're passionate about, but it isn't ready to move on yet. Maybe you know you're missing something, but you don't know what it is. Or maybe you know exactly what you need, but you don't know how to get it. As your vision shapes your view of the world, though, you can start to see opportunities as they arise. But to do this, sometimes you need to pause. You need to put aside your excitement and take time to reflect. You need to listen to yourself and ask: *Is there something here worth exploring further?*

Every now again, put the phone down. Put down the book, log out of the podcasts, turn off Netflix, and do nothing except get silent, close your eyes, and breathe; be with yourself.

Let the ideas pour through your brain like rain. Breathe them in and breathe them out. Write some down; detach yourself from others. Pay attention to what happens in your mind. As a regular daily practice, this process could take hours, days or even weeks, but eventually your thoughts should settle on a few clear choices.

Maybe, after days, weeks, months, or even years, having experienced and contemplated much, earned fresh perspectives and toyed with new visions, you still arrive back at the first idea you had. That's all good—go for it! At least now you'll have some experience to support it.

Recognizing the Opportunity in Front of You

My journey toward Naked Boxer Briefs didn't move in a straight line from a Peruvian night market to sexy underwear on store shelves. Hardly. At first, all I had were some pairs of no-name underwear that I knew were something special. I didn't yet know what my vision for them was, but when I finished my travels, came home and started trying to re-adjust to normal life, my thoughts were always churning on those amazing boxer briefs.

My vision for Naked may have been conceived in that Peruvian night market, but it was born in a hot tub in Abbotsford, British Columbia, a small city just outside Vancouver. I'd been back home for a few weeks, and my friend Kane had his parents' place to himself for the weekend. So naturally he threw a party, and under a clear summer sky he and I found ourselves in the hot tub with a few of our friends and a bottle of Southern Comfort. We started talking, as brash young men do (especially when full of bourbon and trying to impress), and we agreed that it was time for us to step up and make our mark on the world.

It started something like this:

Across the tub, his guests giggling away on either side of us, I saw that Kane's gaze was suddenly distant. He'd always been the artist, the dreamer, and through the steamy air over the bubbling water, I could tell that he was onto something. Another sip, then he looked me square in the eye.

"Let's do something, man."

That clarion call hung in the evening air for a long moment, both of us drinking it in.

"Guys like us," Kane continued, "we were meant to do something great. I know we can accomplish anything."

I nodded slowly. It was like the entire world was open before me, just waiting for me to make a dent in it.

"This is our time," I declared, with all the gravitas my 21 years could muster.

I told him about my idea for this awesome new underwear, and he seized it. We were going to create an entire line of high-fashion men's accessories! By the end of the evening we'd worked out most of the important details, because of course that can be done while drunk in a hot tub, and even had a name for the company (Fredrick Charles—Kane's two grandfathers).

You might think that Kane and I then went on to start Naked. But by the next day, he'd forgotten our conversation and moved on with life. He never shared my vision; it was just the bourbon talking, I guess … something I'd been guilty of before.

But I had a vision, and while he'll never feature in this story again, that conversation with him, with his directness and belief in underwear, helped me to crystallize my vision: I wanted to create high-fashion men's underwear, using only materials so nice you wouldn't even feel them on your skin, and in a style no-one had ever seen before, which I could sell at a premium price.

It might seem that the hot-tub conversation was a non-starter, because the two of us talking never acted on it. But it was hugely important, because my thoughts never wandered far from my vision, and what could have been just a drunken conversation allowed me to vocalize some of my thoughts for the first time.

A good step forward, but was this the opportunity? No. That came a few months later.

By now I was living full-time in Abbotsford. I still worked as a bartender, and also as part of a lawn and gardening team serving the new suburban neighborhoods. But all the time my thoughts were chewing on this idea for an underwear company. I'd learned enough from the embarrassing and expensive fiasco of my failed travel-documentary to keep my ideas mostly to myself, and to not assume that the path to success would be simple or easy. I spent my days trimming hedges and my nights pouring drinks, but I was always on the lookout for that first step on this new path.

It's easy to be excited by your big new idea, and that excitement will certainly fuel your drive to walk down the path. But approach your initial idea with a healthy sense of apprehension and curiosity; let your thoughts turn it over and look at it from all angles. While you contemplate its merits, take some time to investigate the challenges.

For me, the challenges were clear. I was pretty much broke and had no assets, I knew basically nothing about running a business, and I'd never worked in the clothing industry. Enthusiasm and a good idea just weren't enough. I needed something more, but I didn't know what that was. But my thoughts were creating my reality, and I kept thinking, observing, and waiting for another moment or sign that could move the idea forward.

I was paired in my garden-tending duties with a guy my age named Travis. He was easy going, effortlessly cool and we worked well together, and over that summer I learned that he was an aspiring Olympic rower holding down two jobs. He came from a white-collar family but never acted like it—hell, here he was working two jobs at $14 an hour while training every day on the river. This guy wasn't just a dreamer: he made things happen. We became friends over our months working together, and one day I mentioned that I was thinking about starting my own business.

Travis was intrigued by my idea, and since he'd actually paid attention in his Business 101 class he started asking me very practical questions about how I'd set up and run an actual clothing company. Over the next few weeks, the daily monotony of hedge-trimming turned into something much better than a Business 101 class. It was the Council of World Domination as I explained my vision for business success and Travis asked the practical questions. My naivete told me there would be some challenges, of course, but no challenge seemed too great for a pair of 22-year-old comrades with big dreams and a willingness to work hard.

But up until now it was still just a discussion. Neither of us had committed anything, and the vision remained nothing more than an idea we were tossing around. The idea still lacked a critical spark, and we had no idea how to get started. But I was always thinking, and it was always on my mind.

The August afternoon sun was blazing down as I dropped another armload of ratty, thorn-infested brush into the trailer. Sweat trickled through the dirt caked on my arms, and I took a moment to catch my breath, staring down at my t-shirt. There was no way I'd ever get all the dirt and sap off it—another piece of clothing I couldn't afford to replace headed for the garbage once this summer was over. At least my skin always scrubbed clean. Honestly, I thought, this job would be easier if I could do it ...

Naked.

Travis dumped his own pile of brush into the trailer.

I stared up at him. "I've got it. I've got the name."

"What?"

"Naked."

It rang in my ears like the sound of angels printing money.

Travis nodded slowly. "Naked."

It was as if time stood still on that quiet Abbotsford cul-de-sac as Travis and I smiled at each other.
Then my mind started to race. We needed to get this thing going, now.

"There's a local fashion show happening at the end of next month. We need to be in it. We need Naked to be in it."
Travis was right with me. "But first ... We'll need some boxers made."

There were precisely two fabric stores in the greater Abbotsford area. Travis and I took one pair of the sacred Peruvian ginch to the first little basement store and searched for a matching fabric. We found a cotton-lycra mix that was close enough, and bought ten meters of it.

Raw materials in hand, all we needed now was a seamstress. Nobody our age knew how to sew, and beyond the odd button not even our parents' generation could help. But as in so many ways, the Greatest Generation was there to serve.

Travis' grandma knew how to make underwear.

Two weeks later, we were standing backstage at the Abbotsford Hospice Fundraiser fashion show. All the luminaries of the town were there, and as I peeked out from backstage I saw a sea of grey hair, navy blue sports jackets, and modest hemlines. This wasn't exactly the Milan fashion scene, and I'd half-expected there to be an opening prayer before the fashion show got started. I might have laughed, if I wasn't so nervous—was Abbotsford really ready for Naked Boxer Briefs?

I fiddled with the elastic waistband, feeling a ripple of goose bumps rush over my exposed skin. The embroidered words "Naked" looked great, but watching Travis pace around backstage in nothing but the brand-new boxer briefs, I knew something wasn't right.

But just beyond that curtain was the waiting crowd, and the world reveal of Naked Boxer Briefs. I didn't like this feeling—*everything* had to be right.

The show was already underway, and I could hear rounds of brief applause, punctuated by good-natured laughter, over the steady beat of the background music.

I pulled at the waistband again. It was a tight fabric, and the word "Naked" looked cheap and distorted. The rest of the boxers looked great. But today we were on stage—it only mattered what the boxers looked like from a distance. And that, I suddenly realized, was the problem. The overall style wasn't what I wanted.

Although realizing I was obviously and intensely staring at my friend's junk, I forced myself to watch Travis as he continued to pace nervously. Travis' rowing career had carved a lean body of solid muscle, and the boxers were nothing if not complimentary. But they looked too … traditional. Not different enough. Not sexy enough. Not naked enough.

"Dude," I said, interrupting Travis' pacing. "Fold over and tuck in the waistband."

"What?" Travis turned, eyes widening slightly as he watched me flip my own waistband down inside the boxers. He quickly rolled back his own waistband, and I immediately saw the improvement. "Yeah. That's the look we need—seamless."

Travis was about to comment, but was interrupted by the approach of a pair of flushed, grinning, middle-aged women. It was Linda and Caroline, the organizers of the event.

"You kids ready?" Linda asked. "You're on in two."

Travis nodded, and motioned for our dancing entourage of lovely local models (okay, they were our friends from the bar I worked at) to get ready. The three girls shed their bathrobes to reveal their Naked-branded t-shirts under unbuttoned, men's collared shirts, black panties, and long, bare legs supported by super-high heels. They each donned their sunglasses and black hats to complete the look of sultry, sexy dominatrices. It was wonderfully tacky and shameless, not to mention putting the cart a great deal in front of the horse, but it made a bunch of makeshift pairs of underwear feel … real.

"Thanks, ladies," I said to Linda and Caroline, fighting down the butterflies in my stomach. "This is gonna be fun."

"I hope so," Caroline said. "After this we'll either be praised for years or run out of town."

And so Naked Boxer Briefs were introduced to the world. And by "the world" I mean a few hundred local, conservative—and yet surprisingly open-minded—Abbotsford residents. By all accounts our act was incredibly corny and wonderfully amateurish but after months of pondering, dreaming, and working through hypotheticals, I was heading down the path. It was a huge, bold, crazy step out, but it was the opportunity I'd been waiting for. There was an awesome name for the brand. I'd found an amazing business partner whose strengths complemented mine. I had a Peruvian example of the underwear from which we'd created some prototypes. And we'd put it all together in time for the one big fashion show of the year in our hometown.

Sometimes when you look back at an opportunity you realize that it was even more perfect than you thought. Our fashion show appearance was successful, I think, because it wasn't in a big city. Had Travis and I tried to launch that silliness in a place like New York or Los Angeles, we probably would've been laughed off the stage by an audience actually expecting something professional. But Abbotsford was a smaller community—not so small that everyone knew everyone, but not so big that any urban snobbery had set in. Abbotsford was still willing to let local folks just "do their best" no matter how cheesy it was, and they embraced us and our dream with good humor.

Linda and Caroline weren't run out of town, and I think it's safe to say we were the talk of local society … if only for an evening. I'd seized the opportunity, and chosen my path.

Realize That There Will Be Costs

Up until now I realize that I've been speaking in a really positive tone. I make no apologies for this, because anyone considering an entrepreneurial lifestyle better have an optimistic outlook. Understand that once you've chosen a bold path, there will be costs. It's important to recognize this up front and consider the potential costs to you. There will be financial costs which most of us can foresee, but there could be other costs as well.

As Henry David Thoreau said, "The cost of a thing is the amount of what I call Life which is required to be exchanged for it, immediately or in the long run."

When it comes to pursuing your vision, expect there to be costs in your life. Relationships will suffer as you devote more time to your vision. Friends will fall away and your time just "living your life" will evaporate into late nights trying to solve the latest conundrum or meet a deadline. Creating and building your vision into concrete ideas and then into reality is a discipline that requires focus in order to be successful and, at least for a time, you'll be consumed with the work it demands of you.

Where are you in your life right now? Do you have money to invest? Are you prepared to spend the nest egg you've worked so hard for to start a business? Do you own a home and, if you're cash strapped, are you prepared to re-mortgage it? Are you an "all or nothing" entrepreneur? Are you REALLY sure you want to do this? If this is a light choice for you, then you probably aren't taking it seriously enough.

Do you have children and a spouse? Are you prepared for how your selfish actions (yes, entrepreneurship requires you to be selfish with your time) will strain these relationships? Are your loved ones prepared for it too? Talk to your spouse or partner about it, because they're making this sacrifice right alongside you.

What about the lifestyle sacrifices? The comfort of the bi-weekly paycheck will likely go out the door for a while. The cocktails, craft beer, and pedicure budget, if there is one, may get cut down a notch or two. Are you ready for that?

To do anything great requires a sacrifice of your time, your energy, your other desires, and likely some of your mental health.

Consider the worst possible outcome you're prepared to withstand. For some, that may be bankruptcy (no biggy, right?), for others, the threshold may be much lower. This is a deeply personal decision (or a collective decision if a spouse or business partner is involved).

You should have a healthy fear of all of this—one born of an awareness of the consequences of your choice to pursue your vision. If you're not in some ways afraid of your vision becoming reality, then you don't truly know what challenges await. There are no easy paths that are also worthwhile.

Another, more subtle risk is what economists call *opportunity cost.* If you choose one path, other paths may then be closed to you. If you're really dedicated to pursuing your own vision, it means you'll have to say no when someone else invites you to be a part of their vision. The cost that comes with commitment is the missing out on other great opportunities while you work away at yours.

For me, as a 22-year-old single guy, I actually didn't face too many non-financial costs. I didn't have a family so I could spend all my time working on my ideas. I didn't have a house to risk as collateral, or a promising career to give up. At the time, I would have loved to have had all those things, but I see now that being free of any other commitments was actually a big part of the opportunity. I was still mostly wearing my friends' hand-me-downs, drove a piece-of-shit car, and shared an apartment with two other people: basically, I had nothing to lose by launching Naked when I did.

If you're like how I was then, and just starting out in life, you'll definitely face challenges of not having the money, experience, or connections to get a business started—but you'll be free to throw yourself into your vision without sacrificing family, home, or career.

Conversely, if you're approaching your entrepreneurial vision later in life when you're more established, the risks are reversed. You might be in a better position to get funding, to make wise decisions, and to use your network—but beware of alienating your family, risking your assets, or threatening your current career.

So ask yourself: are you choosing this path for the right reasons? Is manifesting your vision worth the sacrifices, both known and unknown, you'll have to make along the way?

You'll exchange a great deal of your life for birthing this idea into the world. Is it worth all this to you?

If the answer is still a resounding YES, then ask yourself just one more question: Why? Why are you doing it?

Why you're doing this is more important than what you're doing.

We'll talk about implementing the why of your business into your product and culture later, but right now, you need to take a breath and self-assess this at a personal level.

Do you want to make money? Great! Is that your why? If yes, is that because you were poor growing up? Is it because Mom and Dad valued money, or inversely, didn't value it? Or, do you just want to provide yourself and your family with a comfortable life?

Will accomplishing your idea give you a sense of self-worth? Would you feel unworthy if this idea never amounted to much or no-one liked it?

Did you discover a problem—something people need—that you want to solve?

Is being famous your big driver? Why? If so, how might that affect you and your relationships?

Do you want to control your own schedule, write your own rules, and not report to anyone? What happens if you take on investments with shareholders and boards of directors? How will you fare in an environment where you're accountable to others?

Maybe you just want to see if you can do it—see if you can summit the mountain. That's a good enough reason as any. Or, maybe you just feel like creating for the sake of creating. Also a great reason!

Do you have a higher calling to help the world in some way?

These questions are important to ask yourself and seek counsel on—with an actual counselor, mentor, or just a trusted friend. The answers to these questions are a reflection of your ego—your sense of self—and they'll undoubtedly be tied to your business or idea. If you can start your business with a fierce self-awareness, you'll be well-served to ensure your decision-making is guided by solid fundamentals and careful consideration of the information you have available at the time—and not your ego.

Recognize Your Vision – Then Act!

Once you've decided with complete conviction and every fiber of your being to pursue your idea, you're going to have to take a leap of faith. Trust your gut feeling that your idea will work out. Be prepared for a huge learning curve. Take it one step at a time. Some people may think you're crazy; most people will focus on all the reasons why your idea won't work. It's your job to focus on your vision coming to fruition. Trust that it will work.

YOU are the variable in the path to creation and the success you seek. You are the alchemist that will turn lead into gold.

Dark times lie ahead for an entrepreneur building a new business. At times, your faith will be the only thing that shines light on the project. To do this, you should believe that the manifestation of your idea is a foregone conclusion. You'll have to maintain a positive frame of mind because your belief, combined with your effort, is the fuel that ignites your idea and keeps it burning.

Although no one knows exactly where inspiration comes from, I like to act as if the idea already exists. "Aha" moments of inspiration feel so powerful when they first hit that they vibrate down to your very core. Every fiber of your being feels that this idea is already real. This is your version of Michelangelo's "I saw the angel in marble, and carved until I set him free."

Another possible step in making your idea a reality is creating some public accountability for your plans. Even if it's just telling your friends. Many people don't want to discuss their ideas until they're fully developed. They may be afraid someone will steal them, or that they'll fail and everyone will know. It's embarrassing to fall on your ass in public. But, if you're afraid of the opinions of others, you have no business being a creator. I've personally found that continually talking about something with like-minded and honest people keeps me accountable and on my path.

It's a fair question, though: how do you know if you've made the right choice?

The truth is you don't. You won't. There are no guarantees. But you must carry on creating and building anyway. The more you create, the less certain you become, and so it perpetuates. There's no telling where all this may lead. Upon taking action, the initial idea may very well transform into another idea. Although these ideas may be completely different, they are inextricably connected—born of each other. I'll talk about the details of getting started in the next chapter, so I just want to pause—with the vision. My vision for Naked grew slowly, as I broadened my perspective through experience, had a few false starts, and let my thoughts become my reality. But when opportunity struck, when I had a brand name, a partner and a looming fashion show, I made that leap. There was a hell of a lot I hadn't done or didn't know yet but I turned my thoughts into actions, and started turning my vision into reality.

2

Taking the Leap

There are dozens of reasons why you shouldn't do something. But as an entrepreneur you need to discover the reasons why you *should*.

Many of the reasons for not doing something are quite practical. So practical in fact, that few would fault you for choosing to not start a new business venture. Here are some common reasons to not start a business:

- *I can't afford to invest in a business right now.*
- *I don't want to give up a regular pay cheque.*
- *I don't want the financial risk of a bank loan.*
- *I don't like how 12-hour days would affect my work-life balance.*

Fair enough. But as you consider these reasons and others, ask yourself this: are they true, or are they just created by fear? Whenever we face the unknown, fear is a natural response—but it isn't always grounded in reality.

And then there are the influences from society that can shape our decision-making. All our lives we're told who we need to be, who we should be, what we can and can't do. When we were good at something, we identified with it, and we appreciate any praise we received. When we were bad at something, we also identified with it, and we remember any punishments we received. Depending on how much fear we feel, the bad memories can sometimes overwhelm the good ones.

These parts of ourselves that scare us, that shame us, that intimidate us, that tell us what we can and can't do, grow from how we've learned to view ourselves based on feedback we've received from parents, friends, teachers, TV, social media, and other people and groups throughout our lives. Our ego takes in and sorts through the information, then creates the construct of ourselves we operate within—the mirror with which we see and define ourselves.

Whether we're aware of it or not, these thoughts create our self-prescribed limitations—the "ceiling" if you will—that block our ability to ascend to our highest potential.

Maybe we don't believe we deserve to be successful because someone told us we'd never be. Maybe we believe we don't deserve to be happy because our parents weren't.

Getting past your fears

In order to break through these fear-based thoughts we have to take a leap and smash through the ceiling to find out what's truly possible for us.

As Gay Hendricks says, "… if I cling to the notion that something's not possible, I'm arguing in favor of limitation. And if I argue for my limitations, I get to keep them."

History is filled with pioneers who smashed through glass ceilings. A classic example, given my love of running, is the story of Roger Bannister breaking the 4-minute mile. "Sub Four," as it's called in running circles, was believed to be physically impossible; however, once Roger Bannister shattered that belief by coming in at under four minutes, others were also soon able to break their own limited beliefs about that once impossible barrier … Now almost every year a new high-schooler runs the mile in less than four minutes.

What's your personal Sub Four? What limit do you currently believe is forever beyond you? Take the time to recognize your fears and your perceived limitations. Are they real challenges, or just a question of attitude? Fear can be healthy when it makes you move cautiously, but too much fear and you stop moving forward at all. The only way forward is to overcome this fear through action.

Taking the first steps

The truth is often not that we're afraid of failing to reach our limits. Our deepest fear, as Marianne Willamson says, "is that we are powerful beyond measure."

The secret to achieving what we deem impossible is, in many cases, quite simple. You don't have to take a GIANT leap. Instead, start small—but carry a big goal. Small leaps go a long way in building greater self-confidence and self-trust in what you can achieve!

Think of each individual leap as your own mountain top—you want to just keep climbing, but not topple over the edge. Be careful not to reach too far too fast, because you might not be ready. Just like a runner who over-trains can get injured and never reach their goal, you too can go too far initially and not recover. Train hard, recover, then train a little harder. This will be highly individual for each entrepreneur, but the principle is the same. Take little leaps, one at a time, and see how they support your ultimate goal.

Here are some fundamentals that can get your business going:
- Open a business bank account and deposit $1,000 dollars in it.
- Join a local association for your business area.
- Find a mentor.
- Study those businesses which are your closest competition.
- Create a basic business plan with a budget.
- Buy a trademark.
- Design a prototype with makeshift components.

Whatever they are, take your first steps one at a time. They might come quickly or be spread months apart, but be sure to respect and recognize each step.

Some of these steps don't come with much risk, but sooner or later you're going to have to take the first real leap. What's the difference between a step and a leap? I'd say a leap is when you have to make a serious commitment of money. Now the risk is real.

My first leap was a surprise—in that I never saw it coming until the chasm was stretching out before me and I found myself standing in the shaking ground at its edge.

I was dangling over a fifteen-foot wide hole beneath a Vancouver street, holding a long, snaking hydro vacuum. Equipped with harness and hard-hat I was slowly lowered into the abyss while six other City workers in reflective vests and polo shirts looked on, thanking God that they weren't the ones about to be knee-deep in sewage.

The stench was overpowering, and I flapped my hands involuntarily in front of my face, unable to stop my relentless descent. Even so, I couldn't help but laugh. Two days ago I'd had two investors lined up for Naked, and yesterday both had bailed. Today was the day I was supposed to be running an exciting start-up with a salary—but instead I was the grease man, or swamper, for the City of Vancouver, forty feet below the busy streets.

My humor stumbled on as I realized that the greatest opportunity in this job would be to get some kind of minor injury, allowing me to kick back on Workers' Compensation. Until that kind of good luck came my way, though, I was getting paid just a little over minimum wage to settle my boots down on the slippery floor as the sewage sludged past my knees.

The hose stretched out before me, quickly lost in the foul darkness. I radioed up that I was in position. Moments later the hose stiffened as suction began to flow, and immediately I felt the pressure as the first of the shit water rushed upward. Now it was just a matter of keeping the hose steady.

The phone in my pocket buzzed. Hooking the hose under one arm freed the other hand to reach in and grab it.

"Hello?"

"Hey, Joel." It was Travis. "Listen, we got a bit of a problem. Hey, what's that sound?"

"Hold on, dude, can it wait? I can barely hear you and I'm standing in three tons of shit water."

"No, this is serious. You're going to want to hear this."

"Really? Okay ... hit me with it."

"We didn't get the trademarks. All our applications were denied."

I was too shocked to reply. Only when the hose under my arm started to rattle and vibrate dangerously against my chest did I realize that it had lifted above the surface and was starting to suck air. If I didn't get the hose back in the sewage I'd be getting sprayed—I'd learned that the hard way once before.

After the hose was re-positioned I forced myself to relax. We'd applied through our lawyer to trademark Naked and its various brand items months ago—that was supposed to be solved.

"Why not?" I asked.

"Apparently some lady in Toronto already owns them. I looked her up and I can't find her anywhere online, so I don't know if it's some kind of small, local store she owns or what. But she owns the word Naked."

"So ... what do we do?"

"I talked to the lawyer and he said we have a few options. We can argue that our application isn't an infringement of her mark because ours is different enough—that'll take six to eight months to resolve."

"And can we still use the marks in the meantime?"

"If we get caught, we could get sued. Our better bet is to file a trademark cancellation to say that this lady isn't using it. She then has sixty days to prove that she is."

"That could get messy. Can we just offer to buy the marks from her?"

"Yeah, that's the third option. We could pay cash, offer her royalties, or even just ask nicely."

"I vote for asking nicely."

"Yeah." Travis paused, and I could hear the defeat in his voice. "The lawyer said he spoke to her on the phone and she didn't strike him as the type that would give you the mark just because she liked the color of your eyes. So he said we should make an offer. He's confident $15,000 will do it."

I felt sick, and it wasn't from the sewage up to my knees. Where on earth was I going to get another $15,000? I'd already maxed a credit card in the legal fees just to get to this point!

My arm was getting tired from supporting the pulsating hose. "Look brother, thanks for letting me know. I'm working right now—I'll call you as soon as I'm in the truck."

Travis signed off and I pocketed my phone. I took the weight of the hose with my other arm and tried to take a deep breath while ignoring the foul air. I looked around in disgust.

"Shit."

The Naked name was everything to me. Without it I didn't want to be in the underwear business. So, despite not having the funds, I told the lawyer to make her the offer. The next few days were a flurry of activity. The lady in Toronto initially put up a fight, but then finally agreed to sell me the marks for, just as the lawyer had predicted, fifteen thousand dollars. I called everyone I knew who might have money to lend us—which at that point was a list I could count on one hand—and basically begged.

I'd already scheduled to meet the lawyer and drop off the cheque, but it wasn't until the night before, pacing back and forth in my kitchen office, that my mom's then-boyfriend (now husband) called and said they'd lend me $15,000.

I felt a little shameless taking the money. Also, my company wasn't even off the ground and was already tens of thousands of dollars in debt. Not what I'd envisioned, but at least most of that debt was almost interest-free and with flexible repayment terms, and it gave my company the trademarks it needed. It was a leap, and it was the first scary leap I took, but it paid off.

But it was just the beginning. There were many more steps—and a few leaps—still to come.

Judging how far to leap

Years later, while building my third startup, we were methodical with every decision we made. We surveyed customers and conducted deep SEO (Search Engine Optimization) research before launching products. Then, once we were ready to launch, we did a crowd-funding campaign on Kickstarter to pre-fund and pre-test the idea. Note, this was the process in my third startup—Naked didn't unfold that way.

I'd converted my apartment kitchen into an office. There were two long foldable tables with a chair each and a giant white board on the wall, with pictures and clippings pinned up for inspiration. If I ate at all, I ate working. Each night after I'd finish a bartending shift I'd sit down and pull out my box of Naked Boxer Brief prototypes. From that pair in Peru to my attempts at removing a waist band entirely and any seam what-so-ever (because what would be more

Naked than no waist band or seams, I thought), there were multiple prototypes from China, Vancouver and elsewhere around the world. Most were terrible!

At first, I didn't have any factory relationships so I'd just Google places and ask them to make a sample. Receiving the mail became my greatest thrill, because in it would either be a new fabric I'd requested or a factory sending me a sample.

Then I learned of a family friend who was a design student in Vancouver and she generously agreed help make a product Technical Specification package and design pattern, based on the design we wanted to achieve. Prior to meeting her I didn't even know what those things were. I'd just send a factory a sample with a bunch of notes—which probably explains why nothing ever came back the way I'd wanted it.

I also found a local fabric supplier with a perfectly smooth and soft "Naked-feeling fabric," and a high quality clothing factory in Vancouver. All of this together helped us finalize a product that Travis and I were actually happy with—a product that looked and felt Naked!

At least, it made us happy. But (pay attention, dear reader) we hadn't yet asked anyone in the industry or the buying public what they thought. Getting the opinion of our target market hadn't really occurred to us—we were so confident that we just wanted to get out there and launch!

On the plus side, Naked's newly sourced Italian fabrics, Canadian production, environmental certifications, and packaging all struck a chord with customers looking for a new take on men's underwear. The $42 price tag did not.

Naked was one of the very first brands in the trend for better quality men's underwear, but some subsequent brands were able to capitalize on our mistakes (such as pricing) and grab the market share from us.

Keep this in mind as you consider how quickly to roll out your idea. You'll be excited about it and you'll always worry that someone might beat you to market, but racing to the starting line doesn't mean you'll win. Google was the eighteenth search engine to enter our world … but they were by far the best.

The more little leaps I took in the early days of my business, the faster my idea propelled into a reality.

But, as excitement was building and so was my self-confidence, I jumped on an opportunity the business wasn't ready for and it led to some rather unpleasant results.

Through an old friend, Travis and I were connected to the producers of Dragons' Den, a long-running Canadian TV show, very similar to the American Shark Tank, where entrepreneurs make business pitches to celebrity businesspeople. Looking back, we were nowhere near ready to present Naked to the world, but this seemed like just too good an opportunity to let pass. So, after a lengthy phone interview which Travis and I mostly bluffed our way through, we found ourselves flown to Toronto, standing under the hot lights of a TV studio, facing the five Dragons.

The sole woman, Arlene Dickinson, was in the chair right of center, a stylish, red leather jacket highlighting her red hair and its signature shock of white. Winning Arlene was the key to this pitch, we knew.

To Arlene's left was Jim Treliving, a restaurant mogul, and to her right were Robert Herjavec, Brett Wilson and the infamous Kevin O'Leary. Keeping O'Leary's caustic tongue quiet was also a key part of this pitch.

I clasped my hands behind my back to keep them from shaking. I could feel my heart pounding, but I managed a cool smile.

Beside me, Travis began to pitch.

"Hello, Dragons," he said. "My name's Travis McLaren and this is Joel

Primus and we're from Abbotsford, BC. Our company is Naked—the new boxer brief."

Arlene's eyebrow rose at that. With a quirk of a smile she started jotting on the pad beside her.

"And we're here today," Travis continued," to offer you a third of our company for only a hundred and fifty thousand dollars."

That number hung in the air for a moment, then I launched into my own scripted intro. I reminded the Dragons of no less than three now-famous underwear and apparel start-ups that had previously appeared on the show, and had been rejected by the Dragons: Ginch Gonch, Saxx, and Coreshorts. It was a dismal list for the Dragons, but it sent a clear message about how they should be looking closely at Naked.

"I was the only one," Arlene said playfully over catcalls of other Dragons, "who tried to make a deal with those companies."

"And no-one would join you?" I laughed, locking eyes with her.

"No-one would join me." She shrugged, still smiling.

The rest of the Dragons let the moment pass and returned their cold attention to the pitch. I forced my gaze toward each one of them, keeping the smile plastered on my face. There wasn't going to be any friendly chit-chat—it was time to get serious.

"What is it that you want?" I asked the entire panel. "You want …"

"Money …" growled O'Leary.

I gestured at him. "You want money. And now it's time for something exciting for you guys to get behind."

Right on cue, the two local girls we'd hired to help us strolled out in front of the Dragons, wearing some tight black t-shirts and black panties we'd quickly whipped together just for this occasion.

Arlene started to laugh, and all four of the male Dragons watched in attentive silence as the girls swayed up, handing out all of the remaining samples of Naked boxers in existence, presented in all five of the prototype box packaging that had been made. I wasn't going to admit it, but I realized that the entire asset list of the Naked company was now literally in the hands of the Dragons.

The girls took their position standing next to Travis, and I cast a big smile at the panel, who suddenly looked far less severe. It was time for the big reveal.

"Okay," I said. "Now this is exciting. But you know what? Let's just get naked."

To a burst of laughter from Arlene, I began pulling off my shirt. The sweat from my nervousness made the fabric stick and the sudden heat of the studio lights bore down on my exposed skin. In my life I'd probably never felt quiet so naked. Travis was stripping too, and the Dragons were all grinning.

"Oh," Jim Treliving said, "here we go."

"You guys are totally sucking up to Arlene," Robert Herjavec exclaimed. "And you know what? It's working!"

Without hesitation, I dropped my jeans and stepped out of my shoes. Travis did likewise.

If they wanted a show, they were getting one.

The Dragons were openly laughing now, and teasing Arlene as she openly stared. I felt a renewed confidence.

Arlene shook her head and laughed again. "You have my attention."

"You know," Herjavec said, "one day I want to invest in a cool underwear company, and make money."

I tried hard not to grin—this was going to be like shooting fish in a barrel. "Well, now's your chance."

 "Okay, let's get to the truth and stop screwing around." The spell was suddenly broken by O'Leary's voice.

In the center chair of the panel he had the commanding position, and all the Dragons settled down at his words. All eyes went to me once again.

Arlene tried to jump in, but O'Leary cut her off. "Arlene, this is clearly not worth four hundred and fifty thousand dollars."

"Why not?" I snapped, suddenly tense again.

O'Leary turned back to me, indignation flaring. "Why not? Because you're a couple of kids from small-town BC, with nothing."

I felt my cheeks flushing. Getting into an argument with O'Leary was the fastest way to get destroyed on this show. I bit down my retort.

"But it's a great idea," Travis said, directing his comment at everyone, "and with a name like Naked …"

It was lame, but it dispelled the sudden tension. O'Leary shook his head but said nothing further.

Arlene was examining the packaging, turning the box over in her hands. "Are you selling any of this right now?"

That was a question we'd prepped for, but we'd just that morning met with the Hudson's Bay Company, a national department store, who'd agreed to take a few sets of underwear as a test.

"No, we haven't," I said, "but we just signed a deal with The Bay."

It was a pretty big exaggeration, and I felt a pang that it'd come back to bite me, but it got the reaction I wanted. Eyebrows rose, and more notes were made.

Arlene was running her fingers over the fabric of the product. "What's the deal with The Bay?"

I had their attention and I had to capitalize on it. I always kept Richard Branson's motto near to my heart: fake it till you make it.

"They just want the men's line for now," I said, thinking quickly. "Uhh, it's … they want to put the product in their downtown locations." I thought about stopping there, but it just wasn't close enough to the truth. "Pending a marketing presentation."

"Are they testing it?" Herjavec asked.

"No," I blurted, fumbling to find the words. I couldn't lie—that would destroy trust. I could exaggerate, but not lie. Reining my mouth in, I admitted the truth. "They're taking it on contingency."

Herjavec nodded stoically. Arlene's smile disappeared.

I could feel the sweat trickling down my back. Dammit. I should have come clean from the start. I could feel the momentum slipping away.

O'Leary scoffed. "So, you don't have a deal. You've got The Bay to look at some samples."

"Yes," I forced myself to meet the glare, "that's correct."

Next to O'Leary, Brett Wilson finally decided to speak.

"Okay, I'm a little concerned that you called that 'a deal'. And I have a few other questions." He glanced down at his note pad. "Have you guys actually done any research into the underwear market?"

"Yes," Travis replied immediately. "And we know that our product is unique in the market."

Wilson tapped his pen against the pad. "How many competitors are there in that market? Answer me that, before we go down any further. How many players are there that own a hundred percent?"

I glanced at Travis, hoping desperately that my partner had the answer. How many players in the underwear market? How was anyone supposed to know that?

Travis was silent. And he didn't have my tendency to grab answers out of the air.

"Well," I said, praying my mind would come up with a good way to finish the sentence, "the Canadian underwear industry is worth a hundred and eighteen million …"

Wilson stared back at me. "Yeah …"

Travis finally stirred himself and threw out a few more industry numbers, then brought it back to the familiar ground of the business plan.

"Our plan calls for us to capture half a percent in Year One." He was visibly shaking, his words struggling out. "Increasing to two percent by Year Three."

Wilson wasn't being distracted, and he brushed aside Travis' words like an errant fly. He stared at me and repeated the question. "How many players sell into that market? I'm going to tear you apart on your two-percent forecast, but let's go back. How many players are there?"

I shifted on my bare feet. Travis was the numbers guy, and I didn't have a clue. The silence began to stretch out, and none of the Dragons were going to break it.

"That's a good question." I heard Travis mumble beside me.

Brett Wilson still stared at him, waiting for an answer. I could see O'Leary shaking his head.

"To be perfectly honest," I finally said, throwing my hands out, "I'd have to say … lots."

"Or," Wilson said, "the other answer is you don't know." He then proceeded to berate us on our clear ignorance of our own market, concluding his tirade with something I've never forgotten:

"You're delusional."

I shut my eyes for a moment, fighting down the upswell of emotion. My gut was like ice. My confidence dripped away with every bead of sweat.

"You have," Wilson added, "no clue."

I'd heard that sort of thing too many times in the past. A tiny fire suddenly lit inside me, and I knew I wasn't going to be kicked off this show by a bully firing random questions at me. So what if I didn't know that specific answer? Survival instincts were kicking in and that voice in my head was squeaking out through what seemed to be its last breaths: *your business vision is amazing, and the Dragons need to see it!*

"We have a great idea," I said.

"You have a wild-ass guess," Wilson interrupted.

I forced a smile to my face, biting down my anger while petty thoughts churned through my head. Who was this guy? Did he live in a world of numbers? Wasn't this supposed to be a show about funding early stage ideas? Where was the vision? How was he ever successful with that kind of thinking?

The silence descended again. Arlene glanced over at O'Leary, who was leaned forward in his chair, frowning. Wilson had sat back in his chair, pen tapping against the notepad.

At the far end, Robert Herjavec was looking down at his own notes. "I can't see a hundred and fifty … I don't know."

That was an opening. I relaxed my stance and looked over. "What can you see?"

"For a hundred and fifty … I'd have to own the business-"

"For a hundred and fifty," Travis blurted, "that's—that's your share of the company. And … with that, we can show you what we can do with it."

It was a bold, almost desperate, claim, and I saw immediately that it didn't impress the Dragons. And I suddenly understood why. I heard Travis' words as the Dragons were no doubt hearing them.

The Dragons, I realized, were far more than just rich people. They were serious investors who'd made their fortunes betting on the right companies. Looking at the hard eyes staring back at me, I knew that my only hope was to sell the dream to those Dragons who could bring their own knowledge and experience in to help. That meant Arlene, most of all.

"The valuation is absolutely insane," O'Leary said. "I would have to own you—all of you—your homes, your cars, everything." He was infamous for his ability to shred entrepreneurs on this show, and he was now grasping for the words to put voice to his contempt. Eventually he just threw up his hands and sat back. "No, I'm out."

I took the rejection stoically. I'd never liked O'Leary anyway, and he'd never been the target investor. Herjavec still seemed to be considering, and Arlene had been silent for a while. If I could offer them a larger piece of the pie they might still invest—but first I needed to get rid of the other naysayer.

With renewed confidence, I glanced up at Wilson. "Brett?"

For having flayed us so publicly, Wilson was surprisingly subdued in his response. "I can't get there with the value you see. I'm out."

The way was clear for the other Dragons to jump in and make Naked their own. Time for the final pitch. I took a deep breath, recovered my smile, and launched again.

"It's not a matter of looking at the valuation. It's also about wanting to be a part of something."

"But it is about the valuation," Herjavec objected. But he was still smiling.

"Okay, in part it is," I conceded, "but we came out here and we said that we need help. We have a product that's ready to go to market, and we're asking-"

"What you did," Herjavec said, "is come out here and say you have a company that's worth half a million dollars. And that's the challenge."

That was an opening to drop the price, I realized, but I wasn't going to do that yet. Herjavec was interested, and Arlene was looking comfortable again. I held my ground and looked questioningly at Arlene.

She shifted in her chair and rested her head in one hand. "I'd want to own one hundred percent of the company, and pay you guys a royalty. And I'd be prepared to put up half the investment, but just in services."

Arlene was a marketing guru—having her services would be no bad thing. But I wasn't giving up my entire company. There had to be room to negotiate. I waited.

Herjavec looked up from studying his notes and spoke over to Jim Treliving at the far end of the dais. "Jim, what are you doing?"

Treliving had been very quiet throughout, which I realized might be no bad thing; any objections to the pitch would have voiced by now. I wouldn't have expected an old restaurant guy to go for an underwear company, but a new flicker of hope ignited.

"I don't know what I'm doing," Treliving said thoughtfully. "You guys go ahead."

I watched the three remaining Dragons. Herjavec was staring down at his notepad. Treliving was deep in thought. Arlene cast her gaze back and forth between them.

"Okay, guys," she said finally, "I'd like you to go into the little back room, so we can talk."

Travis and I headed back across the main stage and into the strange little section of the set where entrepreneurs were occasionally banished. They let us stew in there for a while, before calling us out again to basically give us one last lashing on national TV. We left Toronto with no deal, with no money, and no further forward toward our dream. We'd leaped way too far, and landed (or, rather, crash landed) exactly where we should have, based on our level of preparation and experience. It was a humbling experience.

Things looked so bad, in fact, that Travis decided soon after to give up on our dream. I can't say I blame him—with a degree, a supportive family and his many natural talents, he had a great career waiting for him in the "regular world" and at this point in his life the entrepreneurial chaos ultimately wasn't for him. We parted as friends, but now I was carrying the entire burden of the Naked dream on my own skinny shoulders. I doubt anyone looking at the situation from the outside would have been optimistic.

But if there's a bright side, at least that episode of Dragons' Den was one of the most popular ever, or so we're told.

This story isn't meant to say you can't ever make the occasional courageous decision to put your idea out there—even if the decision is a little ahead of where the business is at the time. But only take a big leap if you've made every possible preparation to do so. Research the heck out of it, consider the worst-case scenarios, and listen to your gut. Then, if it still makes sense, leap.

Learn how to trust your gut

Even if you take a methodical approach to establishing your business through customer surveying, product testing and soft launches, chances are, when you look back after a year or more, most of what you expected to happen will not have happened the way you thought it would. It's a process. It's an evolution. An adaptation.

Leaps, empowered by a base of good data, are then fueled by our instincts. But they're also at the mercy of chance.

The *I Ching, a.k.a. Book of Changes,* offers a healthy argument about the quality of our decision-making. At first it might seem that relevant data should be the sole driver to inform decisions. We're in the age of Big Data and the ability to research before making any choice. *The Book of Changes,* however, reminds us that our great plans are constantly interrupted, if not completely undone, by incidents we can't foresee. Further, if we never stop collecting data and keep trying to predict every nuance and possible outcome, the time when we should have acted will have come and gone.

Ultimately, it's not the collection of valid data that cinches our decision; we have to make the choice to do something—to take the leap.

Personal power lies within your ability to trust yourself. To listen to your instinct (or intuition) and let it guide you. This is age-old advice. Our heads are full of the information we've collected but it's our hearts and our "gut feelings" that provide the compass of how to use that knowledge.

"Trusting your gut is trusting the collection of all your subconscious experiences," says Melody Wilding, a licensed therapist and professor of human behavior at Hunter College. "Your gut is this collection of heuristic shortcuts. It's this unconscious-conscious learned experience center that you can draw on from your years of being alive. It holds insights that aren't immediately available to your conscious mind right now, but they're all things that you've learned and felt. In the moment, we might not be readily able to access specific information, but our gut has it at the ready."

If you can't trust yourself, why should investors, customers, and employees trust you?

After Travis decided to leave Naked I was scared, because I realized how much I wanted this dream to become reality but that I couldn't do it on my own. I needed someone to replace Travis as my partner—someone who had the right skillset for a fledgling company but also someone who cared as passionately about it as I did.

Travis and I weren't number-crunchers, so we'd already been doing some work with another guy a few years older than us named Alex McAulay, who was just finishing up his training to be an accountant. Alex was an incredibly smart and driven guy who I knew from my track and field days in high school. In addition to being a track star (and unlike me was the cool guy sitting at track meets in trendy clothing and with a GQ magazine), he'd been elected as the youngest trustee in the history of the local school board—he was a guy who was going places. He'd helped us out with some of the early financial details of Naked, and when Travis left he expressed interest in maybe stepping up his involvement.

I was intrigued. I liked Alex, but honestly didn't know him that well. In our running days he'd gone out of his way to lend me books he deemed important and he'd introduced me to visualization and mental toughness techniques—skills that shaped my running and life. Given he was older and outside of our regular training and competing, we weren't exactly hanging out on weekends, but he was a friend and someone I had looked up to. He had the skillset I needed, but I had to wonder if he'd really stick around if a high-paying accountancy job came his way. I'd met plenty of people who were big talkers, but not many who's actually stay with a project when it got hard, scary, or potentially expensive.

The more we chatted, though, the more I realized that Alex might be an accountant by trade, but he was an entrepreneur at heart. He was more financially, operationally, and managerially inclined than I was, but every bit the dreamer with a healthy appetite for risk.

There was a lot of uncertainty in giving Alex a stake in the company for such a crucial role, and if I got it wrong my entire dream was at risk of failing. But deep down, I thought Alex was the right person for Naked. Ultimately, I had to make a gut decision. So Alex became the other half of Naked—a position he'd hold with gusto throughout all the trials and tribulations to come.

"As soon as you trust yourself, you will know how to live," said Johann Wolfgang Von Goethe.

The challenge with trusting your gut is that you'll need to ignore many voices both in your head and around you to do this. Your parents likely have a viewpoint on what you should do (or at least they probably did at some time). So will your investors, advisors, co-managers, industry analysts and experts … there is so much noise out there that makes it easy to second guess yourself.

Seeking advice or getting a "gut check" on your plan is important—but second guessing yourself is a dangerous habit.

1. Take time in quiet to reflect on your choices. I will say this

again and again throughout the book.
2. Be aware of your feelings. Scan your whole body and see how you *physically* react to certain things
3. Write down the times when listening to your gut worked out well for you
4. Write down the times when not listening to your gut didn't work out so well.

I'm not suggesting you should use cracked tortoise shells, yarrow stalks, tea leaves, and coin tossing to decide the fate of your start-up, but I share this as inspiration to propel you to trust yourself to move your business forward, knowing you don't have to know everything to take the first step. Do the very best job you can until you've learned more. Once you've learned more, you can do more.

Judge each opportunity, then burn the ships

In the year 1519, Hernán Cortés arrived in the New World with six hundred men and, upon arrival, made history by burning his ships. This sent a clear message to his men: There is no turning back.

Much like the conquistador's exploration, your business will feel like a new world—unknown territory with many obstacles to overcome. Without a ship to return to your former self, you'll have to be fully committed to facing these obstacles head on.

You might be itching to do this from the outset. "Burning the ships" and dedicating yourself fully to your endeavor will feel like the ultimate leap, and it can be exhilarating: just don't do this fresh out of the starting gate. Telling your friends, investing some cash, or acting on the other suggestions I made above all provide a good amount of initial "skin in the game." There will be more flesh to come.

What I'm driving at specifically is to keep a second job or a side hustle that pays some bills and helps fund your start-up for a period of time.

I offer this advice for multiple reasons.

One—Try to fund as much of your own idea as you can until you've proven your concept. The idea becomes more valuable the more you develop it. The more valuable it is, the less ownership of it you'll need to give up should it require future funding.

Two—In those early days when you're writing your own cheques, you'll feel it in your wallet—and probably in your gut as well. Hence, "skin in the game" will remind you to keep asking whether or not you really want to keep pursuing this. Potential investors will value that you've invested in your business as well.

Three—Working multiple jobs is an experience that establishes your work ethic, helps you manage your time, and re-enforces just how badly you want this damn thing to happen. Understanding "hard work" as a concept is easy, but understanding "hard work" by actually doing it is what builds your character.

Finally—just because you've *started* a business doesn't mean you've accomplished anything yet. Just because you want to work only on your new project doesn't mean it's the right choice at this moment. Ultimately, your project will require all of your attention, but assess that moment carefully.

Entrepreneurship requires hard work and humility. Even when you can't see a place to land once you leap, and you don't land exactly where you *thought* you would, you'll land exactly where you should. Get up and find a path from there to move yourself and your business forward.

Take those first few steps and know that you have a lot to learn; in the process of pursuing a worthy goal you're not just building a product, a business, or a piece of art—you're also building character.
A cold, hard truth is that this idea may not amount to anything more than lot of incredible experiences and hard-earned lessons. Most entrepreneurs I know rarely hit it out of the park on their first

go-around. Same with artists and authors. Naked was heavy with lessons and light on financial success.

You're an integral part of the factors that will play into your success, but there are many other factors that are completely out of your control. You're not entitled to great customer reviews, love of your product, or making millions of dollars; but the experiences you collect along this journey and the strength of character you build are things no one can take away from you. Ultimately, this is what you're leaping toward.

Before you press on, I offer you verse 2.47 from the Bhagavad Gita: "You have the right to perform your prescribed duties, but you are not entitled to the fruits of your actions."

And if you doubt yourself and feel unworthy of taking that next step, remember that your goal is worthy because it's yours and, for now, it's a part of you. No other reason is needed.

What's the worst that could happen if you take a risk? What's the worst that could happen if you don't?

The most important thing I've learned through my own experiences and that of my mentors is well summarized by Mark Twain: "Twenty years from now you will be more disappointed by the things that you didn't do than by the ones you did do."

Make friends with all your fears and then just do it! Burn the ships. Take that leap.

3

Building the Business:
Basic Principles

Growing up in the 80s and 90s, from what I'd seen, business seemed like a zero sum game: the only goal was profit. The world, however, shaped my generation differently. Maybe it was a convergence of many things: the growth in global travel, the healthier lifestyles people were living, the call to protect our environment, greater access to information, more connection to people, and the acknowledgement of the importance of mental health. Whatever it was, as I became an entrepreneur my business values, principles, and purpose expanded far beyond dollars and cents.

In Start-up Land, nothing is ever a straight line. It's critical that you have some basic principles in place before you start building your business, because things are not going to always go like you planned. If your basic principles are solid and clear, they can act like a compass as you navigate the inevitable surprises and sudden changes.

Think of building a business as like building a house. You need to know your intended result, have a plan—a blueprint—so you know what materials to buy, which workers to hire, the location you'll build in, how much it's going to cost, and how long it's going to take. For your company, this is your business plan.

After you've done that, you start building the foundation. If the foundation isn't properly established, the house won't stand up to shifts in the ground or bad weather and it will wear down: over time, your house will fall down (or your business will fail).

When it comes to building a business, John Doer states, "Ideas are easy, execution is everything." In order to overcome the "noise" of distractions and challenges and stick to the blueprint of my business plan, I built my company's foundation on four pillars which really helped me focus:

1. Establish your company's "Why"
2. Establish your guiding principles and core values
3. Establish your objectives
4. Establish what is essential—personally and professionally

1. Establish Your "Why"

In Chapter 1, I asked you to think about why you were starting your business. This was a personal question so you could get clarity on your own motives. But you also need to be clear on the "Why" of your business—What's the reason for your company to exist? What is its purpose?

Your "Why" is true north on your company's compass.

At Naked, we sold really nice underwear—so nice that it made you feel like you weren't wearing underwear at all. That's all great, but *why* we did it was what inspired our people to hang around in the toughest of times.

It took a while for Naked to figure this out. Deep down we always knew our "Why" at Naked but knowing it and actually being able to clearly verbalize or communicate it are very different. We'd bandied around some ideas, but it was some time before the "Why" finally crystallized.

Alex and I were on one of our many short trips to Toronto, meeting the buyers for national department stores and major boutiques. We'd also been able to visit a few lingerie stores, but most of our hoped-for meetings were just the first point of contact with these stores and thus hadn't materialized into many sales yet—so I was feeling a little deflated about our cash-starved start-up.

Being crammed in our little motel room for a week, especially with Alex's tendency to allow his clothes to sprawl across the entire room, was a pretty good test of our business partnership. The curtains were parted to let in a touch of sunlight, but the world outside was dingy and cold, and hardly inspirational. The steady rumble of heavy trucks lumbering by added to the distant roar of the freeway.

Staying in one of the downtown hotels would never have been affordable, no matter how many justifications we'd conjured, yet as much as I relished in the idea of staying in the Royal York I still whole-heartedly embraced the adventures of a cash-strapped entrepreneur business trip. Alex and I traded off each night between the bed and the couch in our thirty-four dollar-a-night motel sandwiched between a Denny's and what was probably a strip club in an industrial section of suburban Toronto. And hey, the room came with a free breakfast, and by our second day we'd figured out how to stuff enough food under our jackets to stretch through to lunch as well.

Munching on my third sticky bun of the morning, I sat back on the couch and stared up at Alex, who was propped up on the bed with his laptop.

"I think we've landed in this place where Naked has somehow just become about comfortable underwear," I said. "That's not what we set out to do."

This often happened to me when we'd been talking about numbers and projections and market share and profit margins for too long—I needed to fire up the imagination and start talking about big vision. Alex was the yin to my yang and by this point knew me better than just about anyone.

He looked up from his screen, regarding me with a small sigh. "I know. But when we're looking to raise money, it all comes down to the numbers."

"But it doesn't have to," I persisted, leaning forward. "Our first investors committed on pure vision—there weren't any numbers to show them! Somehow we convinced a lot of people to believe in us, and that's what we need to do again."

I truly believed that if we could convey the power or, better put, the empowered vision for the Naked brand, more investors would rally behind it.

I stood up. I wanted to pace, but the room would only allow about three steps in any direction and there wasn't anywhere clear of Alex's shit. So I planted my feet, trying to let my mind, at least, roam free.

"Right now, what are the first words we use to describe Naked?"

Alex responded quickly. "Sexy. Comfortable. New."

"Right. And all our branding has been about making this mysterious, sexy brand that can apply to anyone. But that's not what we set out to do."

"Preach, brother." Alex knew, as I did, that this wasn't exactly a revelatory moment. We'd done what we could, with the money and time we had, to launch the brand, but we always knew this conversation was coming.

"Not everybody's a model," I continued, "and not everybody feels good about how they look in underwear. Maybe it's a mistake to make it all about being sexy. We want to be inclusive for everyone."

"That's why we went with the minimalist packaging," Alex countered. "We wanted to be the anti-CK and not have gorgeous models on our boxes. The whole idea was that anyone could feel good about getting Naked."

I nodded in agreement. The brand's message had been in our heads for so long that it was hard to imagine that we'd missed or misdirected this idea of sexy. The packaging may have expressed an inclusive, anti-CK or Victoria Secret type of message, but none of our messaging had consistently connected back to that.

"Naked is supposed to be more than just clothing," I mused. "It's supposed to be empowering. We want people to feel great about Naked, whether they're wearing it, investing in it, or just seeing it featured in a magazine."

"Do we want them to feel great about Naked," Alex offered, "or about themselves?"

That stopped my train of thought dead in its tracks. He'd hit the nail on the head.

"I think that's it," I finally said, realizing that I, at least, hadn't been seeing the forest for the trees. "That's what we've been trying to do! We want people who wear Naked to feel good about themselves. It doesn't matter what body type they are, what color skin they have, or what their age is. By wearing Naked, they're saying that they're happy in their own skin."

Alex nodded. "Make the brand more approachable. Give people a reason to truly connect with it—believe in it and feel like they're part something … like a movement toward self-empowerment, not the unattainable."

"I love it." I sat down and grabbed my notebook to start jotting these ideas down.

"Let's get this new vision statement formulated for the next round of investors," Alex added.

The specific "Why" behind Naked had always been hiding in the background, but it took a lot of coaxing, time, and a few days cooped up in a motel, removed from the usual distractions to finally emerge with some real clarity: the feeling of "being comfortable in your own skin."

At the time I started Naked, the advertising world was dominated by over-sexualized ads of men and women. I wanted to create an experience where everyone—no matter their age, build or whatever—felt good, sexy, and empowered. Our belief at Naked was that when people feel good about themselves, their interactions with others improved: they'd be kinder, they'd make better and healthier decisions, and overall the quality of their life would improve. That was why we did what we did at Naked. The medium we used to connect our message with our customers was a beautiful, minimalist pair of underwear and, initially, an underwear box that displayed empowering messaging with no idealistic images of perfect people.

Naked was a typical cash-starved start-up. Our "Why" lived more in our internal branding documents and round table discussion than was ever properly executed—especially after our ideas came under pressure from investors and store partners alike. Nonetheless, it was the reason I was excited to wake up in the morning. Knowing just how comfortable our products were, and how happy they made our customers feel, created an indescribable feeling of satisfaction for me and my team.

Holding on to the "Why" is critical; it gives you an edge that can help make your company unique and it keeps you focused on being the kind of brand customers can identify with.

It's easy to get distracted when building a company, but this is especially so in the early days. Be clear about your company's "Why" and stay on target, or you'll get thrown off your game.

Pressure to change can come from the following areas:
- Customers: many will request changes to your products, or suggest other products you should make. I'm a strong believer in receiving feedback: what the customer wants matters. But you need to understand whether that particular customer is your core demographic when you filter that feedback and

apply it (or not). Trying to please everyone is a distraction and can create a financial drain.

- Store Partners: If you're in the wholesale business your retail partners, especially if they're department stores, will often have strong opinions about what you should and shouldn't do. Their customer intel is based on what works for them. Be strategic in what advice you implement and which opportunities you allocate your precious resources to: large department stores are quick to spend your money to suit their own interests. Often, partnering with a retailer can be a win-win, but other times you end up compromising key aspects of your identity to try and capture customers that aren't necessarily suited to your brand.

- Investors: An investor, or potential investor, may offer plenty of ideas about how to operate your business. Don't ignore this opportunity: listen, learn, and assess carefully—depending on their expertise they may have a lot to offer you. I've had many investors who helped me get my thinking back to core themes and ideas. But don't let other people's ideas become a distraction either.

Don't be fooled into thinking that once Alex and I had figured out Naked's "Why" we never veered from it. Despite our moment of clarity in Toronto that helped shape our "Why" it wasn't too long afterward that we landed a big sale with a major, nation-wide department store. We were elated, but the feeling was mildly soured by the non-negotiable request to change our packaging.

What kind of packaging did the store want? Well, it needed a rock-hard, male body on it, of course. Why? Because that's how people shop for underwear.

Carefully, we laid out our reasoning about how our packing and its lack of imagery was what made us unique, but we didn't dare risk losing a purchase order this huge. We even suggested just taking the underwear out of the box and hanging it so people could feel the fabric and see the length and cut without needing a picture. This too was shot down.

Thus, running against the clock, minimal funds and not totally sure how to execute our vision of inclusivity, we ended up settling for— you guessed it—Adonis on the box!

Sure, we tried to make it artful, but it just didn't feel like Naked anymore. The thought of how people might "feel" when scanning the shelves looking for underwear and seeing our box haunted me at night. I felt like a sell-out to our "Why" and that feeling only got worse.

Every so often our department store partners asked us to change our packaging—they said such a regular change usually resulted in a 2% increase in sales. There were so many opinions at the table, expert opinions I didn't want to ignore, that by trying to please everyone our brand image was completely gone within a few years.

Soon our boutique accounts began to call us out on the changes. Competitors with clear visions for who they were started to steal our coveted shelf space. And, eventually, it became clear that customers no longer connected with what Naked had become.

We gave up our "Why" because of pressure from a huge account. And while the decision to change had won us a huge purchase order, the long-term damage to Naked's brand is incalculable. I take responsibility for this decision, and it's a great example of how we learn the most from our mistakes. Naked's "Why" pillar was not the filter I used in making that decisions—money was. It was money we desperately needed, but it ultimately cost Naked more that the money was worth.

So as you build your business, establish your "Why?" early on—and always remain loyal to it. You might suffer a temporary setback or two, but the long-term benefits of creating a consistent brand that appeals to your core market will ultimately outweigh any short-term gains.

2. Establish your Guiding Principles and Core Values

When you're launching a business, just like building a house, understand that it's going to take longer and cost more (maybe a lot more) than you originally thought. To paraphrase Prussian Field Marshall Helmuth von Moltke: "No plan survives first contact with the enemy."

Of course, I don't view launching your business as akin to facing an "enemy," but the point is still powerful. You'll face many different and unexpected scenarios as you build your business. In order to navigate the challenges and make the best possible adjustments for each scenario, your Guiding Principles and Core Values should be established early and understood by your entire team.

Values are qualities or standards that act as the foundation for our principles and guide our behaviors.

Principles are the rules that lead to our actions.

Think very hard about a few key Core Values and Guiding Principles that will help guide your decision-making early—new Values and Principles can be added and/or developed over time.

Here are three Core Values that we used at Naked throughout my time as CEO:

Taking Extreme Ownership

Take responsibility for your mistakes and overcome them.

With humility, our team members admit and own our mistakes and develop plans to overcome them. No blame whatsoever—not even to ourselves. Mistakes and mishaps are communicated with compassionate, solution-oriented conversations. Clear communication and conditions for success are critical. When we're silent in response, that means we're in agreement with what's being said. Failure is okay, so long as we learn from mistakes. You can't always control results, but you can always control your effort and your integrity—that's ownership.

I like to quote an African proverb I've heard: "If you want to go far, go together."

Action: Be honest. Don't gossip—don't talk behind the back of a team member about what they did or didn't do. Don't point fingers and say, "You did your part but so-and-so didn't do theirs." We are the sum of our parts.

Continuous improvement

The desire for continuous improvement in everything we do. We're all on individual journeys personally and professionally.

It's important to find peace and acceptance wherever and whomever we are in any given moment on that journey. Simultaneously, we must also focus on continuous improvement—to be the best that we can as individuals and as a company. This includes our personal lives, our relationships, our goals, products, customer experiences—everything.

Action: Seek knowledge and feedback. Reflect. Apply the lessons you've learned. Do better next time.

Gratitude

We practice gratitude daily.

We must have a commitment to gratitude and allow it to guide our thoughts and actions. Let us be grateful for those who host us in their beautiful cities when we travel; those who cut the grass, take out the trash and make the coffee; those who raised the people who are responsible for our freedoms today. Let's be radical about our gratefulness every single day.

Action: Say, "Thank you" regularly. Check yourself when you're feeling negative about a situation and count your many blessings. Here are some of the established Operating Principles we employed at Naked:

If it's Urgent, Pick up the Phone.

If something is urgent, don't assume someone is checking their email; pick up the phone and call them. You're more likely to have the opportunity to convey your message and/or get a quicker response to your queries. Calling establishes the urgency of the issue.

No High-Stakes Conversations.

When people are afraid to talk to management or colleagues (or friends, children, parents, and life partners), it's often because they're afraid the other person may react negatively. This results in the issue not being immediately addressed, which leads to an escalating tension around that issue. The longer we wait, the higher the stakes feel regarding that looming conversation. Sometimes, sleep is disrupted because of the internal turmoil we experience over a yet-to-be-had discussion. Create an environment where no conversation is a bad one, where no-one fears sharing his or her thoughts.

Don't Hire Assholes.

If someone acts like an asshole inside the company, it doesn't matter how talented they are; they will no longer have a place in the company. By hiring an asshole, you run the risk of creating a culture of assholes—where fear rules, ideas are not shared openly, and people don't engage with each other. If you tolerate even one toxic person, you're showing your team and customers that you allow certain behaviors.

Immediately Eject People Who are a Poor Fit.

It may seem harsh and almost irrational to immediately eject people who don't fit the company culture, but removing them quickly will prevent long-term damage to the company and morale, even if it causes some pain in the short term.

Always Follow the Process.

Following the process keeps team members accountable and reduces errors. When there's a process to follow, and people follow it, it helps you address issues as they arise; you can correct your course and get the desired end-result.

Focus on the Most Important Task First.

Even if it's something you don't want to do, you should always do the most important task first.

Your key principles will probably be different from mine, but it's important to take the time and energy early on to establish what they are. Some of these principles may seem silly at the beginning when you're a company of one, but your key principles will help you to establish the right habits and the right work patterns, which will become part of the company's DNA and will replicate as the company grows.

3. Establish your Objectives

Everyone needs Objectives (even the founders and CEO) and

everyone needs to know what these are. Objectives are usually simple, easy to define and, very importantly, measurable.

A good objective is NOT something like this: "Dominate the market". That phrase may be simple, but it's very hard to define (does domination mean "most recognizable" or "most profitable" or "most widely available", or ...?) and impossible to measure (what does "dominate" even mean?).

A better objective would be something like this: "Get our product for sale in ten Bloomingdale locations by the end of this year with at least two shelves of product per location and a minimum of 25% sell-through per week". That's still very simple (even if there are more words) and it's also easy to define. It's also easy to measure because it's specific, with a certain department store named, a number of stores and a deadline.

Note that this objective doesn't say how it's going to be accomplished—just what the goal is. The person assigned this objective still has a lot of freedom to figure out the best way to do it, as well as the flexibility to try creative solutions if their first plan doesn't work.

Making objectives public (at least within the team) allows everyone to know what everyone else is responsible for, and creates a sense of accountability. It doesn't require a detailed summary of what each team member is doing on a day-to-day basis, but it reminds everyone that each team member has their own area of responsibility that they're working on. Some folks may get to work early; others may stay late; some may be on the road week in and week out, others might never leave the office. But with public objectives everyone can rest assured that everyone else is working as hard as they are: it's the ultimate accountability.

Objectives that are anchored by realistic and agreed-upon timelines keep your team focused on required tasks. Team members will feel much better about the company and their day-to-day work when goals and objectives are clear. Establishing fewer objectives will increase the possibility of success.

At Naked, we established objectives very early on. We borrowed from Entrepreneurial Operating System® to define our key objectives as "Rocks" according to four distinct parts:
- The What—What is our goal? It should be easily understood by all.
- The How—What do we need to do in order to accomplish the objective and what do we need to do to get there?
- The Results—Are there measurable steps we can take along the way that lead to successfully reaching the objective? Establish relevant KPIs (Key Performance Indicators) to measure results that will lead to success in the objective.
- The Reflection—Afterward, we reflected on what went right and wrong with our steps, KPIs, and process. We'd discuss this openly as team members and assess what we might need to change for the next set of objectives.

Here's an example of a hypothetical company's "Rock":

"To raise $500,000 in the next six months to fund the launch of our new women's four-piece collection."

When presenting the Rock internally, the CEO would share the intended use of the raise (manufacturing prototypes, extra sales trips, early advertising, etc.) so the team could understand the benefits of achieving this goal.

The high-level steps to achieving this objective could be:
1. Complete Investor Presentation.
2. Update Company Financials.
3. Ensure Due Diligence package & checklist is complete and easily shareable via private Dropbox link.
4. Ensure company NDA (Non-Disclosure Agreement) is in place.
5. Prepare list of fifty potential High Net Worth Investors, Venture Capital Funds, Private Equity & Family Offices, as well as potential grants that invest in our industry at our stage of growth.
6. Make ten calls a day to prospective investors.

When it came to reviewing our results at Naked, and reflecting on our failures and successes, we always provided an open forum for people to speak. Everyone should have an equal voice.

That said, we did not place a high value on opinions unless they were rooted in facts. This might sound contradictory to Naked's respect-based team culture, but I'm not saying we didn't listen. Opinions can be good, bad, or otherwise, but they're inevitably presented through the filter of our own biased experiences and knowledge—anyone can embrace or reject something based on their own opinion. Instead, we focused on facts. Facts don't lie, and they aren't colored by philosophy: they simply exist. If we didn't have enough information to make proper judgments we'd reach out to our customers, our partners, and relevant experts to help us arrive at fact-based conclusions, rather than just our opinions.

Having dialogues based on as many facts as you can get helps alleviate the emotional twist people can get into when sharing their opinions.

Every three months our team would establish our new objectives for the following three-month period and host daily and weekly calls to ensure we were on the right path.

Our daily calls, which we referred to as "Huddles," were focused on the day-to-day activities of the company. In them we ensured everyone was aware of what was urgent—or "on fire" as we called it—and what decisions needed to be made today. Daily huddles were focused on immediate and essential tasks, which often resulted in team members having to do first what they wanted to do least of all. We had a policy that no decision that could be made today would be delayed until tomorrow. We'd review the Key Performance Indicators of various aspects of our business (i.e., sales, web traffic), and if there were any red flags we'd address those immediately.

On our weekly calls, which we called our "Rocks" calls, team members would update their progress on achieving their key objectives. We always kept our "Rocks" as objectives that moved the business forward in a big way. We installed the popular and simple Red, Yellow, Green Light protocol to assess progress: A "Green Light" response from a team member meant they were on path and no further discussion was needed. A "Yellow Light" from a team member said they were falling behind but were confident they could get back on track. A "Red Light" meant they were behind and stuck, and the team needed to rally around and support them to get back on track.

Setting objectives is a foundational pillar of building a business but it's important to approach objectives with an open and, dare I say, flexible mind. The Marshall Goldsmith expression—"What got you here won't get you there"—comes to mind. Factors change and you need to be able to pivot and adjust your objectives as needed to propel the business forward.

Always hungry for sales, our team created seasonal promotional packaging to entice our store partners to buy a few extra pairs of underwear. We created an Objective to be "the best-selling underwear product in Nordstrom and Holt Renfrew for Valentine's Day".

Here's what we knew going in:
- Our store partners didn't have any additional budget to allocate toward buying more Naked product;
- We didn't have any budget allocation to invest in new inventory;
- We didn't want to risk owning seasonally specific inventory we'd have to "take back" from the stores if we didn't meet our objectives.

So, we created a Valentine's heart-shaped sleeve that beautifully wrapped two pairs of Naked Underwear together. The sales associates could put the sleeves on two pairs of existing inventory, re-merchandise it on a visible shelf and, after Valentine's, just rip the sleeves off any product that didn't sell and put it back on the shelves.

The stores loved it. We asked them what the best-selling brands were doing in terms of weekly sell-through at the stores and made enough

sleeves to sell more underwear than those brands.
Our marketing team had a specific PR objective that landed our little
Valentine's sleeve on National TV—including The View!

Our sales team called the stores and trained the individual department
managers on how to package and merchandise the underwear.
We visited the top stores to ensure that we'd personally trained each
sales associate on the benefits of Naked and even gifted each of them
a pair to ensure they could speak to customers about the comfort
from personal experience.

Our warehouse team had to ensure that all the stores received the
goods and that, because there was no product in the boxes (only
sleeves) and large department stores usually use UPC scanning to
identify goods, these were sent directly to the department managers.

And each and every day, team members met to ensure everyone
was either Green with their objectives or, if not, there was someone
ready to help!

And guess what? We hit our objective—we became the best-
selling pair of underwear during Valentine's in both of our major
department store accounts! In fact, it was one of the best-selling
periods our company ever had—and it was not by chance.

Objectives are an essential tool for any company, as they show
everyone the path you want to tread and what role each team
member is playing. Like guiding principles, objectives may seem
like an unnecessary effort when you're first getting started, especially
if you don't know enough about the business yet to set realistic
objectives—but set them anyway. Even if your first set of objectives
are way off, at least you'll have learned how to set more realistic ones
next time! And pretty quickly you'll learn how to set good objectives
that will motivate, inspire and direct your team.

4. Establish What is Essential

Your business Essentialism (i.e. that which is essential to your business) is established by your "Why" and your Objectives, and it's personal as much as professional. Choosing to focus on what's essential provides us with the time, creativity, and clarity to execute on our business and maintain a healthy balance in our lives while doing it. But our time at the office isn't all that needs to be accounted for. Time spent with family, friends, extra-curricular activities, health, dating, etc., all factor in. All the things we do affect us mentally, emotionally, financially, socially and physically.

I remember the night when what was essential in my life changed forever. I was sitting in my poorly lit bedroom (in the apartment I shared with two other guys), pounding out emails. Should I have been emailing? Probably not. I was in a woe-is-me state of mind, upset about a cavalcade of different problems with Naked which had sparked an adrenalin-charged, long-winded "follow-up" email tsunami to anyone I could think of. Not a great idea.

My phone buzzed and I snatched for it on pure instinct. Was it another angry customer? Or a new sales order? Even though it was already well past normal working hours, in my overworked mind I could envisage little else.

It was my brother, O'Neil, suggesting that we go out for a pint that evening.

No, I texted back. *I'm getting work done.*

Bumped into Alex, came the reply. *You guys are working too hard. Come out for a drink.*

I was in that mindset where I couldn't see a life outside of the business and it seemed to my sleep-deprived brain that I had a responsibility to sit by my computer and solve Naked's problems.

Thanks, I texted, *but I'm too tired.*

I went back to composing my email. Seconds later, the phone rang.

"Hello?"

"Dude, don't be a lame-ass." It was O'Neil, and I could hear the grin behind his words. "It's just one drink. Everyone needs a break—just come let loose with us for a bit, then you can get back to it."

I stared at my screen. I was like a hammer looking for nails and I really wasn't getting anywhere with this email. But maybe I could review our financial forecasts …

"Joel," O'Neil said with new earnestness, "the first one's on me."

Who could say no to free beer? My laugh was little more than a sigh, but I agreed. It was only a short walk from my apartment to the local pub, and in the warm summer air I actually started to feel human again. I found O'Neil and Alex quickly enough, and plunked down at the table as Alex filled my glass from the pitcher.

Alex was looking as exhausted as I was, but a spark of life ignited in his eyes as we listened to tales of O'Neil's latest international adventures, this time in Amsterdam. Alex was keen to travel, I knew, and he asked a lot of questions about how to get around in Europe. I just sat back and soaked in the atmosphere, surprisingly happy to be away from my computer screen for just a little while.

As fate would have it, on the other side of the cosmos (in this case, the cosmos being Abbotsford), a young woman was also being reluctantly coaxed out to the same watering hole by her own friends. She was a nursing student, exhausted and stressed by the tremendous workload, and as in need as I was of a solid night out. I didn't see her arrive, but when I first laid eyes on her I only half-wondered if she'd just descended from heaven.

Even from across the pub, I was arrested by her beauty. Her face was like an angel's (if angels were brunettes and tanned) and when I saw her laugh I felt my own heart soar. Her smile made me forget that any other woman in the world existed, and I knew that I just had to introduce myself. I'm dead serious—this was perfectly corny, Hollywood-level love at first sight … at least for me!

Wait—what? Me, walk up to a woman in a pub and just introduce myself? Sure, I'd strip down to my underwear on national TV, but … this was talking to a girl in a bar—a skill I hadn't improved much since our Peruvian debacle! And I had precisely half a beer in me—not exactly enough to grant me liquid courage.

O'Neil and Alex were still chatting away about Europe; neither one noticed my faraway stare or the sudden churning in my heart. I tried not to stare, but my gaze kept returning to that beautiful woman—even if just to prove that she was real and still there. I tried to reason with myself. It's not like I'd never had a girlfriend or been on a date. If I'd muster the courage then, why not now?

She suddenly rose, and from her body language I assumed she was taking drink orders from her friends before she headed over to the bar. Before I even realized it, I was out of my chair and walking over. My stomach was churning, like it often did before I made a big investor pitch. That thought actually calmed me, and as I watched her speak to the bartender, indicate her table and then start to head back, I told myself that this was just another pitch … as lame as that sounds!

I altered my path through the tables, hoping to intercept her. I had no idea what I was going to say, no idea what sort of "pitch" I was going to make, but I sensed an inevitability to this meeting. We intersected between a couple of tables on the edge of the dance floor, practically bumping into each other as we each navigated past the chairs. She looked up at me in surprise, and a bit of a laugh.

That laugh was all the encouragement I needed. Even if I had no clue what to say.

"Hi," I said. "I'm Joel."

Her face split into a dazzling smile. In her greenish grey eyes I saw an amazing kindness. And maybe just a spark of interest.

"Hi," she said. "I'm Janna."

We talked for hours that night. She didn't give me her phone number, but I'd forgotten to ask … so I paid the price. We chatted on messenger for the next month or so before she let me take her on a date—it was worth the wait. It was the beginning of a lifelong romance, friendship, and partnership. Janna invited me into a world I didn't yet know: one of spontaneity; of late nights (not just working); of time just being together with no schedule. I felt relaxed in her presence and for the first time in years I felt happy. Janna was all about doing small things with big love and from the moment I met her, like an oracle she became my teacher about what "else" is important in life.

As you build your business, remember that you do still have a life outside it. Entrepreneurs need to prepare for this by understanding that:

    A. you can't do all the things you want and give your business the amount of time it needs to be successful;

    B. the time you spend on non-business-building activities should, as best you can, relieve and refresh you, not create additional stresses that then carry over into your business.

You can't control every single thing that happens, but you can certainly make choices about what and who is essential to you, and build a structure into your life that focuses on that.

Some tips on Essentialism:
1. Prior to starting a new project or business launch, review everything you have going on in your life: re-assess your

priorities and remove everything that's non-essential. This ensures your maximum focus is on the task at hand.

2. If you feel it's necessary to step down from other activities, ensure you honor the commitments you've already made. Work closely with the people involved to exit without creating issues for them.

3. What extra-curricular activities are you doing that may need to be dropped? Maybe pick just a few things to help de-stress and refresh, like exercise, hiking, and yoga.

4. Maybe this is extreme, but even go as far as choosing a minimalist wardrobe where you essentially have four pairs of the same pants and six of the same shirts and two of the same pairs of shoes—to remove the stress of having to choose what to wear each day.

5. Building a business that's in start-up phase means you may be more antisocial than you'd like to be. Ensure you're investing time with people with whom you truly want in your life. Accept it when others self-select themselves out of your life if you can't give them the attention they need from you. You simply can't be a successful entrepreneur and be all things to all people. Those who deeply care about you will understand the choice you've made.

6. Learn to say "No." Opportunities will come up all the time. Favors will be asked of you. If it's not a "Hell, YES!" then it's a "No." This doesn't mean you won't be in the service of others. We all need to do our part by giving back to our family and communities, so assess the trade-offs. Ask yourself, "If I do this extra thing, can I do it as well as I could two years from now? Will I be present while doing it?" There will be time down the road to do other things and give more of your talents and effort to others.

7. Establish a routine and diet that optimizes your performance and focus. Routines are sometimes tough to keep up while building a business, but they can also be a major boost to your productivity. What are you eating for breakfast? Does it fuel your mind and body or make you sluggish and tired? How do you start your day? Is it with mediation, exercise, journaling and emails or is it rushing out the door in a frenzy? Figure

out what's essential in your routine to optimize yourself for building your business.

8. Organize your personal space and life. I've found that cleaning up the space around me (my desk, office, even my house) before I sit down to work helps clear my head and prepare me to focus on the work I'm about to do. Before launching a new business, I ensure my personal finances are in order. Do I have tax returns complete so I'm not scrambling if they're requested for a loan or grant or an audit? Do I know what my monthly bills are and does my current monthly budget align with what I may need to run my business? Does my car work well, or might I have unexpected problems driving to important meetings?

On a daily basis, this practice is almost like warming up your body for a big race—the warm-up lets your body and mind know that a concerted effort is coming and you need to be ready. As crazy as it sounds, occasionally I even get a haircut before tackling a project or going on a business trip. Many people I know believe this type of practice is just procrastination. I agree that we can't always have everything "just right" before we start something, but my father always told me that our outward state mirrors our inward state, so it's essential to have stuff in order. I couldn't agree more.

So make sure you figure out what the essentials for your business and your life are, and always keep them central. Life as an entrepreneur is chaotic, busy, exhausting, and sometimes scary—it's easy to lose sight of what's essential amongst all the noise. But if you can keep your essentials close, they'll empower you as you slog through the daily churn of the entrepreneur.

As a final thought for this chapter, I encourage you to remember your Principles, your Values, your Objectives, and your Why as you build your business. Be willing to pay the price for honoring these choices.

What does "paying the price" mean? It will mean saying "No"

more than you'd probably like to, making trade-offs, lay-offs, and sacrifices. Strictly adhering to your Guiding Principles may also mean that your growth takes a bit longer or profits are occasionally lost. Keeping your Essentials at the center may mean you have to pass on an opportunity or two. But you're building something to last and these things will guide you through the challenges you face along the journey.

4

Raising Money

So, you've written a business plan. Established your guiding principles and processes. You've built a prototype. Bought a trademark. Started coding. Found a factory. Did a bunch of research and data mining. Tested a minimum viable product. Wrote a screenplay, recorded an album ... Whatever it is, at some point the thing is probably going to need some cash to get off the ground.

Let me state this right up front: if you don't have to raise money ... don't. At least until you've built some value into the idea.

If you can start your business without investors, then do it. At least for your first one. There are certainly benefits to using other people's capital to fund your business, but initially it's less complicated and more efficient if you can grow on your own. If you're starting your business a bit later in life and you've put away some savings from your day job, that can be your pre-seed capital. Likewise, if your business idea is something which requires no hard spending before sales revenue comes in (say, a services company with no costs for inventory or equipment, etc.) then you might be able to get started by investing nothing more than your time and expertise. But beyond these two happy scenarios, if you're starting a business you'll probably have to think about asking other people to invest in your company.

The good news is, today is the golden age for launching businesses or ideas with minimal dilution (investors diluting your ownership through investment) because you can sell or share what you've built directly with your consumers online. No studio or storefront required. You can buy do-it-yourself, turnkey websites on Shopify and even pre-sell your product on platforms like Kickstarter and Indiegogo (See Appendix).

The first place many of us think to go when we need money is the bank. This is where we get our car loans and our mortgages, and your bank is probably an institution where you've saved at least some money for years. If nothing else, you probably have a bank account. You might think that this is an obvious place to get your seed capital—just show the bank manager your brilliant business idea and get a loan to fund it!

Unfortunately, as I learned as a 22-year-old trying to get Naked off the ground, banks aren't quite as warm and cuddly as their advertising suggests. I walked in with no savings, no assets, and no established career. And no bank would touch me. Why? Because if a bank is going to lend somebody money, it wants to be sure that the money will be paid back—and that requires something called "collateral". Basically, the bank's assumption is that I'm going to default on my loan, so it wants to know that it can seize my assets to ensure it doesn't lose anything.

I'm not going to lie, it was pretty frustrating. As I faced rejection after rejection, I kept thinking: "If I already had a house and fancy job and tons of mutual funds, I wouldn't need a bank loan!" It seemed to me that the banks were only willing to help people who really didn't need the help. Folks like me, who had nothing but a great idea and who desperately needed a loan to get started, weren't welcome at the banks.

So, for any aspiring entrepreneur who needs start-up cash in amounts more than they can personally provide, you're going to have to look elsewhere for the funds. Also, beyond the start-up phase, to really scale your business in the long term you'll often require a lot of subsequent investment.

The reality as an entrepreneur is that, at least for a period of time, raising money may just end up being your primary job. So, let's talk about raising money for the business.

Pitching Investors

Convincing people to hand over their hard-earned money to fund your business dream isn't easy. It's not impossible (I only say that because it will often feel that way, trust me), but according to the National Venture Capital Association (NVCA) *2020 Yearbook*, with data provided by Pitchbook, the US venture ecosystem ended 2019 with more than 10,400 companies across the country receiving venture funding, with approximately 1,300 venture firms managing over 2,200 active venture accounts, and more than $444 billion in venture capital.

Capital is out there for your business but to be successful you need to consider a few simple rules and have the right mindset.

First of all, check your ego at the door, because you have to be prepared to get a little shameless. You have to be mentally ready to find money by almost any means necessary—as long as it's legal! It's also going to be a bit like asking out someone you have a crush on, but don't have a chance with, over and over again—because rejection and raising money usually go hand in hand. There isn't a more soul-crushing experience than sharing your idea, baring your life's purpose, and have someone say it's bad, stupid, or inferior to someone else's. On the flip side, there's also nothing more soul-affirming than getting back up after being floored by a rejection, dusting yourself off and saying: I still believe!

Second, remember that even though you're pitching someone to fund your dream, it's not your dream during a pitch—it's their dream you're appealing to. They want to be part of the next big hit! They want financial freedom, or maybe some recognition for their intuitive power to recognize future success, and they're willing to gamble for it.

Third, be relentlessly positive. I like Neil Pasrichra's tip to add the word "yet" to the end of negative thoughts that begin with words like "Can't." When you feel like you're never going to get a cheque in the door just say, "I haven't raised the money … yet!" Personally, I find it helps to adopt an abundance mindset because it will sometimes feel like there isn't money out there but in fact there is—billions and billions of dollars are being invested all the time. I like to think of money as energy and we energize it with our power and mindset. That said, no matter what you believe around intentional thinking, there's no question that a positive mindset around money and abundance is better than a negative one.

Finally, be ready for the fact that raising money almost always takes longer than planned. You'll have to, as Alex says, "Kiss a *lot* of frogs!" before you find your prince or princess.

I realize this might not sound like fun, or what you're interested in as an entrepreneur. You want to get going on your business, but you need to take the time and perfect your investor pitch. Remember, investors kiss a lot of frogs too and need to be smart with their capital.

Raising money can be a full-time job that'll make you feel like being a prisoner trying to break out of your cell with a single rock. You'll bang that rock against the wall with no progress until one day, finally, there is a chip—you've made progress! So, strap in for the long haul.

And be ready for a few surprises along the way, like the time I was driving through the mountains on the way to an investor meeting with Tim Morgan, one of the founders of WestJet.

Through the Abbotsford Entrepreneurial Club I'd met a guy named Ross who really seemed to get the vision of Naked. Ross had started a couple of small businesses and we'd met many times over the past couple of months to discuss possible strategies for getting Naked off the ground. Ross still had a day job to support the "side hustle" of his start-ups, and that day job happened to be in Tim Morgan's company. Ross was impressed enough with the idea of Naked that he'd mentioned it to Tim, and Tim, amazingly, had agreed to meet with me. So Ross and I piled into the car and headed out to cross the mountains.

We were making good time through the mountain passes, intending to cross the Rockies by sunset and descend into Calgary in time for a late dinner. I was at the wheel and content to focus on the road—while spring had already come to the West Coast, here in the mountains the snow was thick and ice hard to spot. Traffic was light, but enough huge transports had roared by in the oncoming lane to keep my hands firmly on the wheel.

I slowed as we drove into the small town of Golden, nestled amongst the peaks near Rogers Pass. It was a quaint place with charming buildings. Small town Canada was usually depressing in late winter, but not this place. Still, I couldn't wait to reach the bright lights of Calgary.

The traffic lights up ahead switched to green as I coasted toward the intersection, and I tapped the accelerator to pick up speed once again. There was an oncoming car indicating a left turn, edging forward to start its turn once we were clear.

Or not. That car wasn't stopping.

"Shit!"

I hauled the steering wheel to the right as the oncoming car turned into me. I swerved into the next lane, ignoring the horn blaring behind. The oncoming car slammed into my door, jolting me sideways and pushing my entire car to the right. Glass shattered and fell across me, bouncing off my arms as I frantically tried to steer back toward the road. Something punched into the passenger side of the car. The world through the windshield spun wildly.

Then, suddenly, everything was still. Peeling my fingers from the steering wheel, I glanced around at the shattered interior of the car.

"You okay?" I heard Ross say.

"Yeah. You okay?"

"Yeah. But we better get out in case the car catches fire."

There was already the faint smell of smoke from somewhere, and that was enough for me. Throwing off my seatbelt and shouldering open the door, I climbed free of the wreckage.

The car was wrapped around a streetlamp. In the intersection, three other vehicles were crumpled against each other at various angles.

There was no fire, yet, so I reached into the back seat and collected my backpack with the investor materials, computer, and business attire—thinking it a miracle these somehow hadn't been destroyed. Ross rounded the car and stood next to me. Dark splashes stained the lower part of his shirt and his pants.

I pointed. "You hurt?"

"No," he laughed. "The coffee wasn't too hot."

I shared in the laugh, taking a deep breath of the cold mountain air. Bystanders were already running in to check on the occupants of all the vehicles, none of whom seemed badly injured. Some locals came over to check on us, but I reassured them that we were fine. I felt great, actually. Totally pumped up and ready to get on our way. If the car wasn't so trashed, I'd have jumped right back behind the wheel. Calgary was a-calling.

It wasn't until the police and ambulance arrived that I noticed my whole body was shaking.

I had to admit that the policeman's insistence on Ross and I going to the hospital was a good idea. Once the adrenalin rush faded, I began to notice pain in my back, and a quick examination revealed a huge gash just below my shoulder blade. Smaller cuts from the exploding window glass had striped my forearms like a tiger's, and apparently one of my teeth was chipped. The doctor sewed me up, cleaned and bandaged my arms, and took a few x-rays just to be sure. The service was professional and efficient, but even so it was evening before we finally emerged from the hospital.

The air was frigid under a clear black sky, brilliant stars shining down over the dark silhouettes of the mountains. Wrapped in my West Coast jacket, I shivered and realized that the faint tingling in my back and forearms suggested that real pain was on the way.

Ross adjusted his backpack with his one good hand—the other was bound in a brace due to a seriously banged-up wrist—and glanced left and right across the dim parking lot.

I caught the instinctive motion, and realized that I too had been vaguely scanning the parking lot, looking for something.

"Dude," I said, as the full weight of reality suddenly hit me, "we don't have a car."

Ross turned to face me, breath wafting around his face. "What time's the first meeting tomorrow?"

"Eleven, I think."

Ross looked around again, scanning the faint lights of the town of Golden. "Let's get some food. We have some thinking to do."

There was a highway pub on the far side of the parking lot. It was warm and it served quick food. And, even better, martinis—something to ease the pain a little. We chowed down the local fare with surprising speed, and it wasn't until the second round of martinis that either of us turned to the new problem at hand.

"Calgary by eleven o'clock in the morning," Ross mused as he watched the olive dance in his swirling glass. "And no car."

"We could hitch-hike," I suggested. "I made pretty good time when I hitch-hiked most of the way across Canada."

"We wouldn't get picked up at night." Ross shook his head. "And we'd freeze walking along the highway."

"We'll rent a car, then."

That seemed like a good idea, but I started to feel sick as soon as I started thinking about actually getting behind the wheel again. I pulled out my phone. "Maybe there's a Greyhound bus or something."

A quick internet search showed no buses leaving for Calgary that evening. There was, however, a bus leaving at five in the morning, scheduled to pull into Calgary in time to get to our first investor pitch.

Ross pondered that. "Leaving at five in the morning? That'll mean wake up around four." He glanced at his watch. "If we can even get a motel room this late."

For me, there was no discussion required. "Then we get up at four. Or we sleep at the bus station if we have to. We are making that meeting."

Ross' face, which had displayed something less than enthusiasm, brightened up.

I leaned forward, meeting my friend's gaze with a clarity of purpose I hadn't felt in months.

"I've spent the last year and a half dedicated to this dream. I've pitched hundreds of potential investors. I've been humiliated on public TV. I've had business partners come and go. I've maxed my credit cards to buy a trademark and consolidate my debts, just to stay alive after having invested thirty thousand dollars-plus into this company. There is no chance in hell that we're not going to make it to these meetings. I don't care what it costs. I don't care what it does to me. I am going to be there."

Ross stared back at me, his face slowly breaking into a smile. "And I'm going to be there with you. Let's go find us some bus tickets."

It was dark and miserable, but we got those tickets and found a place to sleep for a few hours. By the time the pale winter sun rose on the east, we were looking down at the vast prairies and the city of Calgary spread out before us.

Meeting Tim Morgan was almost enough to make me forget the day before. It was almost like meeting a celebrity, a man who'd done what so few others could do in those Great Recession days—he'd built a phenomenally successful airline from the ground up. His swagger was inspiring, his confidence infectious. He was a man who knew exactly who he was and what he was capable of. By the time we finished the initial conversation with Tim and his brother Darcy, I'd decided that if I could ever imagine myself at sixty, I wanted to be just like Tim Morgan.

Our meeting had stretched over lunch in the restaurant of the Calgary Fairmont hotel. The post-crash adrenalin rush was long gone, and I shivered through the pitch, ignoring the pain and stiffness throughout my body. I'd given the pitch hundreds of times, though, and part of it was when I talked about myself and my personal character in overcoming various adversities in life—a little car crash wasn't going to slow me down. The fact that both Morgan brothers seemed genuinely interested was helping, too.

When the bill came, I quickly offered to pay for it.

Tim laughed. "Joel, you'll learn that *most* investors are just looking for a free lunch! But considering you're the one who fought through a car crash to come here and tell us you need a few hundred thousand dollars, I think I can pick this up."

I tried to hide my relief, cringing inwardly at how much brunch at the Fairmont would likely be.

I'd been cold all morning, but I suddenly felt something like sweat trickling down my back. I instinctively tried to turn my head to look, then bit down the pain as my neck muscles refused to move.

"Ross," I said quietly, "I think I've bled through my bandages on to my shirt. Is it showing?"

I leaned forward, elbows on the table, as Ross leaned back to discreetly check.
"No, nothing visible."

"Joel," Tim said, handing off the completed bill to the waiter, "you're looking a little pale."

I forced a smile. "Sorry, just a little stiff."

"We've been sitting for a while—why don't we stretch it out a bit?" He rose, turning to his brother. "Darcy, can you go over the Naked financials with Ross one more time? You have a better eye for the numbers, especially when you're not being interrupted by me all the time."

At Tim's beckon, I struggled to rise and follow him out into the Fairmont's elegant, sun-soaked lobby. We found a pair of armchairs and sat down. Tim dropped his beat-up leather bag on the floor and stretched out his legs. I eased myself down and leaned forward, not wanting to put pressure on the oozing bandages on my back.

Tim's gaze rested on me. It was a hard, penetrating gaze, but in it I saw none of the negativity I'd experienced before from other investors. There was no patronizing sneer just below the surface, nor any sense of predatory duplicity.

"Joel," Tim said simply, "you got a lot of moxie."

"Thanks."

"I like what you had to say this morning. I figure I'm going to invest twenty-five thousand into your company, because I believe in you." He waved his hand vaguely. "There are a few things about your business plan I need to learn more about first, but I've realized over the years that the success of any start-up depends entirely on the person at the heart of it. I think you've got the chops, and I want to help you."

As the Calgary sun shone down through the lobby windows, I felt an inner glow ignite within me, as if the sunbeams were reaching down from God Himself to pat me on the back like a coach and say "Not bad, son … not bad at all."

After so much rejection, after so many pitches to rich people, after the humiliation of the Dragons' Den, this was what success felt like. Tim Morgan, a real-life successful entrepreneur, believed in me.

It was a great start. But it didn't end there.

The slog of pitching

You're going to have to do a lot of pitches, but that doesn't mean you approach everyone with money. You can create a long-list of people who you know have money and a track record of investing, but from that create a short-list of the people who understand your industry. Start your pitches with them, because even if they say no they have the potential to help you immeasurably. They might give you feedback, based on their knowledge of your industry—if so, consider their advice carefully, because it comes from a place of experience. They might also introduce you to new contacts, other people in the industry who might be a better fit for your idea. One of the best things you can hear during a rejection is, "This idea isn't for me, but I know someone else who might be interested—let me introduce you."

When you're first starting out, getting feedback and getting introductions are gold. Welcome them, consider them, adjust your pitch to incorporate them, and move on to the next meeting.

Prepare a business plan that outlines the most important aspects of your business and your strategy for the first three years. It's great to capture the big picture to establish your vision, but you don't want to share too many details unless you're crystal clear and laser focused on how you'll deliver your vision. Otherwise, investors may fear you'll spend money on the wrong things early on.

In addition to the business plan, create a presentation that overviews your company and the opportunity at hand (Appendix Reference). Prepare an elevator pitch (a few verbal sentences) to grab the attention of a potential investor in the shortest amount of time possible. You never know who you might run into in an elevator or at a cocktail party or a sporting event, etc.

Finally, create a financing plan to clearly outline how much you've determined you'll need to raise over the course of the next few years. This way potential investors can see what type of future dilution they may incur and understand the probability of a profitable exit down the road. This also includes having foresight when setting up your capital structure (i.e. the types of shares you and your shareholders have in the corporation and what functions they serve). A lawyer or an investor who helps entrepreneurs structure all different types of capital raises can help you with this.

You have to put yourself out there. Study your short-list, pick up the phone and make appointments to present your pitch. Get on the road and meet people face to face. Apply to Angel Networks and pitch competitions. If you don't have a decent office to invite people to (and given you're a start-up I wouldn't expect you to), pitch in upscale hotel lobbies. These are usually spacious, well-designed and comfortably furnished, and quieter than coffee shops.

Pitching can be uncomfortable, and getting so many rejections, no matter how polite, can be demoralizing. But your dream is counting on you to convince other people to support your idea with money. Ask yourself every day: "What is the one thing that I can do today to raise money?"

When pitching your business, clearly communicate these key things: your objectives; the problem you're solving; why you're the person and this is the idea to solve it; your path to achieving those objectives; and the real value of the opportunity. You believe in this idea: be sure to let that shine through in your presentation—you'll have only minutes to impart that you have those attributes. Be realistic, yes, but also be so authentic and compelling that you'll be hard to ignore.

Create a team that champions your idea—people who are as passionate about it as you are. The more passionate supporters you have, the more other people will feel it's a good investment. But be careful you don't build a cheerleading squad comprised of only friends and family—having accredited investors who've succeeded with a few startup investments can make all the difference in raising capital in those early days.

People know people who know people, so you never know just how important one pitch may be. Always be present, passionate, and authentic with even the most unassuming of potential investors. It's always important to be a decent human being and treat everyone equally—but with investors, you just never know how that might pay off.

For example, three early investors were my three bosses from the jobs I'd worked while trying to get Naked off the ground: the owner of landscape company, the owner of the sewage pumping company, and my manager at the newspaper. These were three guys who had every right to dismiss me as a dreamer, as a nuisance who'd wasted their time by being a short-term employee. But something about my sincerity, my transparency—hell, maybe even my sheer *tenacity*— had made them believe in my dream.

When you start raising money, remember that you're *always* on stage, and that people you might think never even noticed you are paying attention. Be honest, be upfront, and let your passion shine through. You never know what doors might open.

No matter how great the idea is, businesses can fail in a thousand different—and unexpected—ways. Investors know this all too well, which is why part of their decision-making process is to investigate the founder's character and experience—both business and personal. You, as the entrepreneur, are the alchemist that turns lead into gold and injects lifeblood into the idea. You are the person around whom the team and the culture are built. You matter, at least as much as your idea, when it comes to convincing an investor to give you their money.

Just a quick statement about non-disclosure agreements (NDAs). Most investors I've pitched simply won't sign them. Unless your idea is truly earth-shattering and life-changing, don't ask anyone to a sign an NDA. Rarely are people interested in stealing your idea. Most people are good and honest and know nothing about startups or have any desire to start one themselves, especially if they can fund someone else to do the work. If you're concerned about sharing too much, then just give a high-level overview of the idea or business and see where the conversation goes.

Okay, so I realize that's a lot to take in. Especially if you're not interested in pitching people to raise money. But trust me, it's good information to consider because sooner or later you're probably going to have to explain to somebody important what your business is all about. And even if you don't, just going through the process of preparing a complete pitch will help you tremendously in focusing on the essentials of what your business idea really is. More than likely, though, you're going to have to raise money, and preparing yourself for the slog of pitching is an important process well worth your time.

Business Partners

One possibility that may be present when you first start your business is having a business partner. Naked was originally started by Travis and me—we seemed a natural fit and neither of us would have dreamed of moving forward with Naked without the other. But after the first, disastrous appearance on Dragons' Den, we suddenly found that our life priorities weren't as aligned as we thought. Basically, Naked was my life's dream and I was prepared to throw everything I had into it, but Travis had other opportunities—great opportunities—and he no longer thought Naked was worth the cost. We parted ways after just a year, thankfully amiably.

Maybe it was just because I was used to always having a business partner, or maybe because deep down I was scared of trying to do this on my own, but in those start-up days of Naked I always had someone close to me in the business who I considered a partner—complete with ownership of the company. In these tumultuous years of getting Naked going, I learned just how important it is, if you're going to have a partner at all, to get the right person at your side.

I tend to go through life like a sponge, sucking up all kinds of habits and ideas—good, bad and neutral. Naked taught me what kind of people I need around me: they need to be honest, trustworthy, positive, and kind—people who lift me up. I learned through hard experience that I needed to stay away from people who brought me down with negative and toxic behavior.

Business partners sometimes have the luxury of really getting to know each other beforehand, while other times it's just pure cosmic attraction and a gut feeling.

I've seen the most spontaneous and serendipitous of partnerships last a lifetime. I've also seen family members never speak to each other again because a deal went sideways.

Whether you're choosing a partner or a director or shareholders, be patient in making a decision. Observe the consistency of the person's character. Anyone can "put on a show of niceties" for a week or two. Are there red flags? Do they seem genuinely honest or are they inconsistent in temperament? How do they treat other people? If you witness a genuine act of kindness from them, that's a great sign, and I'm not talking about high-fives and calling you buddy or buying you a drink. Do they listen to you and let you finish your sentences? Also, do you think they can take responsibility for their actions?

If you practice listening to and observing these people, you may get a feeling deep in your core about their character. You can certainly be wrong about it—I've been wrong more times than I care to admit. Sometimes you may need to work with someone to accomplish an objective even if their character isn't compatible, but at least if you know who you're working with, you can align your expectations and manage accordingly.

What will lead to successful partnerships has little do with someone's knowledge, expertise, or checkbook. It's about the ethics, fairness, and trustworthiness of the person you choose, your acceptance of them for who they are, and your mutual willingness to work through the things you'll face together

Your partner will be your late-night texting buddy, hotel roomie, seat neighbor on the long-haul flights, the one who shares your dream and, hopefully, who shares the financial burden.

Partnering with someone because you feel helpless and desperate in certain aspects of your business is no different than dating someone because you think they complete you. It's a terrible idea. If you're not great with, say, numbers, you can always hire an accountant or bookkeeper. A partner is much more than that.

Sure, your talents should complement each other. One of you may be a better manager or designer than the other, but you each bring 100% responsibility to the partnership. You're not two halves of a whole. You're each the whole and together your strengths can propel the company forward. You can depend on your partner, but you're not dependent on them. Instead, ask yourself if you augment each other.

I was lucky. When Travis left we had another team member, my accountant friend Alex, and Alex fortunately had enough of an entrepreneurial spirit to jump in with both feet. True, at the time our company was worth nothing and Alex and I presided over little more than pie in the sky ideas, but his passion for Naked was equal to mine, and he brought more than just complementary skills. We became partners in the truest sense of the word, and that partnership became the rock upon which Naked was built.

Partners are there to help each other grow as they strive toward a common goal. They hold you accountable for your bad habits and tell you the truth 100% of the time. And lastly, if you "break up" with them, you need to be that amicably divorced couple who makes everyone else jealous. Meaning, you have so much mutual trust and respect for your partner that you wish them well even if they need to chart a different course for their life. Failing that, get good legal advice on how to structure your partnership agreement with breakup and tie-break provisions in those gleeful early days before anything bad arises. Your shareholders will likely demand, and be grateful for, this!

So keep your eyes open for potential business partners, but be very careful before actually committing to a formal partnership. These relationships matter, for the health of your company and often your own personal well-being, and once formalized they can be hard to end. Trust yourself enough to realize that you can do this on your own—you may not need a partner at all. But if you really do find that perfect person to help you grow the business, go for it.

The Different Stages of Investing

Don't expect the investment journey to be a neat and tidy, well-marked trail. Raising money always takes more time and more effort than you'd expect. For most of us, being creative and flexible (and praying every now and then) will play a big part in figuring out how to finance the business—especially if it's your first start up.

Very important: during this process, don't lose sight of the day-to-day running of the business. Ever. It's a successful business that people will ultimately want to invest in so, as they say, "keep your eye on the ball."

Your first round of capital is usually called Love Money. In other words, for your first cash infusions, you need to go to the people who love you: your family and friends. Why? Because they know your "character" and will likely believe in you before your idea is fully developed. Love Money, though, doesn't mean "Dumb Money"—you'll still have to prove to friends and family that you have the particular skills required, or willingness to gain them rather quickly, to successfully realize your vision.

That said, tread carefully. Your business can fail, and you have to answer to these people for the rest of your life. If you lose their money and they weren't mentally or financial prepared for that possibility, Thanksgiving dinner will suck for the rest of eternity.

Never pressure family members to invest or ask for more than someone can afford to lose. In my native Canada, an investor who is not family or friend must be accredited—which means, based on their yearly income or net worth, they can theoretically afford to lose the money and understand the risks associated with the investing. In Canada that means you need to earn $200,000 at least two years in a row or have a net worth of greater than $5 million dollars. In the US to be an accredited investor your net worth must be at least $1 million.

If your family members don't have experience investing, they may understand they "can lose" the money but may be so excited and blinded by their love for you they may forget just what it means for them to lose that money. Always clearly explain the risk.

If you've successfully acquired an initial round of capital from family and friends, and moved the business a few steps forward, then your Pre-Seed or Seed round of financing is next. Seed Capital is money invested in exchange for equity in a company that's starting up. Investors are providing "seeds" so you can build a foundation for your idea. You've shown the early signs that your product or idea has some market traction (such as, people are buying it or expressing interest) but you still haven't determined just how much you can scale the business.

Often this investment is structured as a convertible note—a short-term debt. The investor, usually known as an Angel Investor, can convert it into a later round of financing once the company is further de-risked by more sales or more investor capital. This structure provides mutual flexibility but predominately gives the investor some added protection if the ideas being seeded don't take.

There are Angel Groups or Forums in most major cities in North America and they often allow entrepreneurs to make pitches through an established vetting process. These forums are competitive and time consuming. You'll not only have to grab the attention of angels who may likely see one hundred investment opportunities a year, but they also demand a lot of due diligence to validate your pitch. Successful or not, though, this process will teach you how an investor looks at your business—a excellent skill set to development.

If your first investment comes in the form of a Convertible Note, remember that you'll have to factor into your business model the repayment of that note. You'll also have to show how exactly you're going to provide these Angels an exit which provides them, hopefully, a healthy (profitable) return on their investment.

Grants are also available to start ups. There are lots of grants available, but they tend to be very specific to industry, stage of business, and even gender. You can spend a lot of time applying for grants and if you're successful it will be well worth it—cash infusion with no dilution … it doesn't get better than that. Just be sure you meet the requirements for the grant you're applying for. In my experience, grant specifications are taken very seriously and if you don't meet all of them you've wasted a whole bunch of everyone's time.

After your first round of Seed Capital is complete, you may also want to do what's called a Series A round of financing within a year or two. This capital gives you the rocket fuel to scale up fast. But don't attempt this raise if the company is still struggling to survive month-to-month. The sort of investors you want to attract for a Series A financing, usually Venture Capitalists or Family Offices, will want to see that you've proven your company's market fit and that the necessary operating systems are in place to ramp up your revenue in a major way.

As I discussed earlier, the banks are probably not an option for an entrepreneur lacking established financial assets. But, don't write them off forever. In your first two or three years of operations, thanks to the Love Money and Seed Capital rounds of financing, hopefully you can build your business to a point where it's generating revenues and, even more importantly, not losing money. If that's the case Development Banks or Credit Unions may be able to provide new financing or banks may provide loans based on your cash flow. You'll likely need at least two years of revenue to de-risk the business enough for a bank, and you'll still have to personally guarantee the loan, but at this stage you'll have a shot at more traditional financing which won't dilute your ownership like additional shareholder funding would.

You may have proven your business, scaled your business, and be quite smitten with all that's happening with your idea, but you're still not finished raising money. Like I said, more often than not it's a job an entrepreneur is never done with.

After all this comes additional rounds of financing (Financing Series B & C), and the possibility of taking your company public (listing it on a stock exchange). But that comes later, when you're probably not a start-up anymore. For now, just focus on the early stages of investing: love money, seed capital, grants and, eventually, bank loans.

Valuation of the Company

Something really important to understand is the fact that every time you give an investor shares in your company, you're giving up some of your ownership. Every start-up needs cash, but you as the founder need to consider very carefully what you're willing to give up. In Naked's early years I made hundreds of pitches, and sometimes I'd be offered an investment big enough to solve all the company's problems—in exchange for a majority share of the company (and sometimes the whole company!).

In every case, no matter how dire our financial situation was, I declined. I always needed money for the company, but I was even more determined to make sure it remained my company. It was my dream—I wasn't going to just sell it off. I had to learn quickly how much my company was realistically worth, and how much of it I was willing to give up. It made for a lot of unsuccessful conversations with potential investors.

And then, out of nowhere, I got invited to back on Dragons' Den for a re-pitch. And yes, even after the televised smackdown of my first appearance on that show, I accepted. Because a lot had happened since then, and both I and Naked were very different.

The waiting room in the CBC studios in Toronto was pretty much the same as last time. The eclectic acts around us this time ranged from neon-colored gymnastic equipment, a couple of dudes with guitars, and a whole family on wheels with a variety of fuzzy safety helmets.

I was in business casual with a leather jacket, nicely contrasted by Alex in his snappy blue suit. We had a whole troupe of models with us this time, men and women, and the best of our retail packaging, including the Valentine's Day special two-box set.

Alex was visibly fidgeting, reciting his spiel to himself as he tried to take deep breaths. It didn't help calm my nerves. I knew my business inside out, and I'd defended it so many times over the past year that I didn't expect to be surprised by any question. I knew the market, too, and knew what it took to get into stores and to make real sales happen. It was less than two years ago that Travis and I had stripped down on the set for our public humiliation. But it seemed like a lifetime had passed since then.

We got our call, and headed for the studio. Fueled by a rush of fear, I strode down the catwalk and bounded down the stairs. As my feet touched down on the floor I once again spotted the five Dragons, seated on their curved platform, stacks of cash piled neatly beside each of them.

Arlene Dickinson was in the center seat, and her face lit up warmly as I caught her eye. To her left Kevin O'Leary offered his usual scowl, and next to him Jim Treliving was as stoic as ever. On Arlene's other side was the new Dragon—Bruce Croxon, the founder of Lavalife. com—and beyond him was Robert Herjavec.

Without even thinking I waved, as if I'd spotted some old friends. "Hey, Dragons, good to see you again."

Arlene smiled and returned the greeting.

"Good to meet you guys," offered Bruce Croxon.

"These are underwear guys," Arlene purred. "Naked, if I recall."

I reached my mark on the floor and planted my feet, noticing Alex appear at my side.

"You may remember us," I said with a big smile, "as the guys who tried to pitch you Naked Underwear." I gestured to my side. "This is my new business partner, Alex."

"What happened to the old business partner," Kevin O'Leary asked.

I shrugged broadly. "Travis decided that it just wasn't going anywhere. So we had to re-think our business plan, re-model, and start fresh. Alex is a CA and," I laughed, "I have my own limitations. I think Alex balances out those limitations with his knowledge."

This drew approving nods and smiles.

"Okay," said O'Leary, "so now we got CA and The Kid. Are you guys like a band, too?"

"Or a train robber gang?" added Herjavec.

The whole mood in the scene seemed pretty light.

It didn't make me feel any more confident, though: the Dragons had been smiling before they destroyed us last time. I nodded to my partner. "Alex?"

Alex cleared his throat. "Dragons, today we're here to offer you 17% of our company, for two hundred and fifty thousand dollars."

O'Leary laughed out loud, but even he was writing down the figure with the others.

"Good for you guys," Arlene said. "I hear you've had some real success since last time."

"Now I want to get things started right," I said, grabbing my lapels and pulling my jacket half-way off, "so this whole thing is about getting naked ..."

Arlene's face lit up in anticipation.

I slipped my jacket back on. "No, just kidding."

Her expression dropped almost comically. "Oh, Joel, come on …"

"We got a little bit of cash now," I laughed, "so let's bring in the models!"

On cue, our five models strolled out, showing plenty of skin as they handed samples of the product to the Dragons. As planned, the dude wearing nothing but the skimpy briefs offered the package to Arlene, and she was almost blushing beneath her laughter as she accepted. The other Dragons didn't look quite as impressed, but I saw a few eyes following the female models as they paraded slowly by.

"So," I said once everything had settled down again, "we've been picked up in Holt Renfrew across Canada, and more than thirty independent retail stores. And most of them are high-fashion boutiques. So far, it's only the men's line of underwear that we've launched, though, and we're looking for additional investment to develop and launch the women's line as well as t-shirts."

"Joel," Bruce Croxon said, "I'm a Stanfield kind of guy. I wait for the two-for-one sale at the Bay and I don't care what kind of underwear I've got. I could not care less—so could you do me a favor and get right to the business of it? Are you going to make any money this year?"

"Fair enough," I replied, "let's start there. First off, let me tell you what we've been up to …"

"Numbers," Croxon growled.

"What are the sales?" O'Leary asked.

I caught myself, nodding. "A hundred and fifty thousand, so far this year."

"Okay," interrupted Croxon, "so three, four hundred thousand this year."

"About that."

"What do you make on those sales?"

Croxon was being pretty belligerent, and I actually paused for a moment.

"Profit is 45%," Alex offered. Croxon tried to keep going but Alex stole the initiative, addressing all the Dragons. "Before we go into that, I think it's really important to understand where we're going with the product lines, because what you have in front of you is only one style of underwear, and that's definitely not—"

"Wait, wait," interjected O'Leary. "CA Guy, one second. The last time this dude was here," he gestured at me, "he blew his brains out with a ridiculous valuation. Now you're profitable, supposedly, and you want us to pay nine times cash on an underwear company?"

"Before we do," Alex said, "I think it's a better idea to start with the vision of where the company is going."

"Forget vision—that's bullshit! We're talking about a multiple of cashflow here."

I shifted my feet, listening as Alex, the accountant, started getting into a debate with O'Leary and then a few other Dragons about the importance of vision and future plans over present-day cash flow. There was some laughter, but I could tell that the Dragons were starting to think that Naked was still just a dream a couple of neighbourhood kids had put together in the tree fort.

Arlene Dickinson kept pushing down the growing sarcasm of the others, I noted. Her interest was real, and it was enough to overpower the cynicism of O'Leary and Croxon. Robert Herjavec was very quiet this time, and Jim Treliving said as little as usual, although in his hard gaze I could see something I liked.

The argument eventually wore itself out, and a long moment of quiet descended on the set. I forced myself to retake the initiative of the conversation.

"The fact of the matter is, we're in talks with Nordstrom. We've had two meetings with their national buyer and we're looking at a fifty-door, million-dollar sale."

"Tell them what the Nordstrom buyer said," Alex added, "about the product, the quality."

"He picked up the underwear and he said that it was the nicest underwear he'd seen."

A couple of dragons were taking notes. All cynicism seemed to have vanished.

"I'll make an offer," O'Leary suddenly said. "You know, I'm going throw out an offer because you're just such a tenacious guy." He was smiling, and for the first time I sensed, maybe, a glimmer of respect. "I'll throw in fifty grand to a two-fifty valuation equal to 50% of the company. I don't ever want to go to board meetings or any of that crap, though."

Half the company. I didn't like the sound of that. I did, though, like the sound of an investment from a Dragon!

Alex glanced at me, whispering something that sounded positive.

"I really like Joel, too," Arlene said, studying the Valentine's Day package. "But, I don't know ..."

Croxon restated his disinterest in underwear and said he was out. It didn't fuss me at all. The other four Dragons were all clearly still interested.

The discussion continued, with Alex fielding most of the questions now. I was watching the Dragons and was liking what I saw.

"The key to it," Jim Treliving suddenly said, "is that it's a great product, with a great name."

"So, are you in?" O'Leary asked.

He considered. "Yeah, I think I could throw fifty grand at this. Robert, how about you?"

"To me," Herjavec said, "it's a flyer. I don't mind losing fifty grand on it—I believe in this kid."

"Arlene, what about you?"

"I really want to be a part of this," she said. She locked eyes with me, her expression thoughtful, almost sad. "But I'm not sure if 50% is the deal you're going to want to do. I'm torn."

I was torn, too. The Dragons were offering us real money—and real respect—but they were just asking for too much. Arlene had nailed it. And looking back at her, I shared her sadness.

Alex nudged me. "We should talk about this."

I broke Arlene's gaze and refocused on the group. "Can we talk about whether we'd want this deal?"

"Of course," Treliving offered.

"Go into the rat cage," O'Leary barked with his old menace, "and come back when you're ready."

We walked to the little cell at the back of the stage. I held the door open for Alex, and a cameraman, and followed them in. The cameraman gave a thumbs-up.

"They believe," I said, finally releasing my amazement.

"They do believe," Alex replied, face all business. "But if they're talking 50% we have to go in with a higher number."

"They won't go for a higher number."

Alex frowned. "So, do we walk?"

I shook my head. "I think we're close. Maybe not with O'Leary but with the others. We can deal."

"We need to get as big an investment as we can—it's all about the cash."

I hesitated. Alex was right: at this stage in the company's growth it was desperately starved for cash and not much else mattered.

But it mattered to me. I just didn't want to hand my company over to anybody just yet ... but I really wanted to work with the Dragons and be done with raising money!

"I won't give up more than 25%," I said.

"That's not enough cash," Alex countered. "It's hardly worth it."

"But they won't go higher, because O'Leary's framed it as a multiple based on sales to date."

My frustration was building. Were the Dragons—and all investors—really nothing better than the banks? If it's safe I'll give you my money, but if there's risk you're on your own. It doesn't matter that fifty grand is your life's savings and to me it's a rounding error ... It wasn't fair. Why were people always looking at past performance, even in start ups, and not future potential?

"I got it," I said. "Let's offer 25% at our valuation, but contingent on us signing the Nordstrom deal."

Alex pondered that. Then he nodded. "Let's do it."

We emerged from the cell and walked back out into the lights. There was a new tension in the air—a sense of expectation.

I presented the counteroffer. O'Leary was out almost before I finished saying it. Herjavec followed shortly thereafter.

Arlene, however, was impressed. "I like an entrepreneur who's willing to risk everything until he delivers what he promises. To me, that's a guy I want to bet on. I would do that deal."

All eyes turned to Jim Treliving.

He tapped his pen against his notebook. "How about we make it 30%?"

Arlene's face broke into a grin. Alex was clearly trying to keep a smile off his face. But I didn't feel like smiling. Nearly a third of my company handed over. With the investors already on board that would reduce my personal ownership to about 35%. And there would be more board members—more people telling me what I could and couldn't do.

"I couldn't live with less than that," Treliving added, "and if you can't accept 30%, then I'm out."

Alex looked hopeful, but pained. He waited for me to make the call.

I was glad I hadn't eaten much, because my stomach was churning. I could hardly believe my own words as I said them. "I can't do thirty, Jim, I'm sorry."

Treliving's face was impassive as he nodded.

Arlene shook her head. "I'm really, really sorry, but I have to be out."

I wasn't surprised, but it was Alex's despondent face that hurt the most. For the second time, I turned and walked off the set of Dragons' Den with nothing.

Except, perhaps, my pride.

I share this story because it's important to understand the valuation chasm—especially before the business has a proven track record and scalable business model—between the entrepreneur and the investor. No matter what stage your business is at there will be give and take on valuation and your vision needs to be backed by evidence—evidence O'Leary and Croxon wanted to see in the form of "numbers" and proof of traction.

As the founder you need to own meaningful equity in your idea, even if your idea requires a lot of venture capital. By meaningful equity I mean this: enough equity that you still feel like A) you own your idea, and B) that there's upside in your equity should you sell the company or take it public (list it on a stock exchange). Without meaningful equity it's easy to start feeling like your company is just like any other job, and you'll resent the endless hours you're putting in to build a company that isn't yours anymore. You may have founded it, but if you don't own enough of the company to matter, then why are you doing it?

That said, it is YOU that needs investor capital. And sometime the cost of that capital is greater than you'd hope for.

Maintaining meaningful equity is closely wrapped up in the concept of valuation: how much is your company worth? This matters specifically when you're offering shares in the company for investment dollars, because quite literally you have to put a price on each share. In very simple terms, if your company is valued at

$100,000 then a person investing $20,000 now owns 20% of the company. As the founder, who can see the vision and who carries the passion to succeed, it's only natural that you'll place a higher valuation on the company.

To an outside investor looking for a solid return on their money, though, it's only natural that they'll place a lower valuation on the same company. Or maybe, more fairly said, a valuation that can realistically provide them a return on their investment.

Exit plans

Remember that an investor is looking at this deal with the end in mind. You'll need to do this as well. Even if the thought of selling your business seems strange right now, a path for how you're going sell it, or provide liquidity for your early shareholders, needs to be built into the plan. Will you uplist the business on a major stock exchange so your shareholders can sell their shares? How much time and how much revenue do you need for that to happen? Will a venture capitalist or private equity buy out the existing shares at a value greater than they paid?

Or will you merge with or sell your business to another company? If another company is going to buy your business, at what stage of your growth might they do that? What technology or market segment do you own that they might need, and how might you structure your business to increase their interest?

As these are all questions very specific to your business and industry there's no one size fits all approach. The only point I'm stressing is that you'll need to communicate this plan from the beginning to convince investors. Hopefully, you're starting see why I said at the beginning of the chapter that it's simpler to not take on investment if you don't have to.

Finding the right valuation

Once a company is up and running, with two or more years of solid business data to examine, valuation can get a little easier because it can be pegged to something tangible, such as annual revenue or annual profit. Most start-ups won't have seen a profit in their first two years, and to be fair investors understand this, so valuation will more likely be based on revenue.

Valuation gets trickier, though, with a true start-up—a company that's little more than a good idea ready to get started. In most cases and sectors, pegging a valuation to an idea that has little to no actual financial traction is challenging, and venture capitalists have every right to put a high value on their cash. This is where you can do research on other companies in your industry and see what valuations they raised money at and how much revenue they had at the time. They're called comparatives or "Comps" and they're critical for establishing and defending a valuation.

But assuming you've done proper due diligence on the opportunity, executed the early stages of your product and tested its market viability, don't undervalue yourself either. Yes, I know you're desperate for cash, but investors are hungry for great ideas as well.

Try to find investors who understand your business sector. These investors will better appreciate the value you're trying to provide them. For example, if you're starting a restaurant, an investor who primarily invests in mining or technology may not have the appropriate references or experiences to understand why your restaurant is something unique or exceptional (or may not be able to assess the risks and opportunities well enough to be comfortable parting with their precious cash).

Furthermore, speaking with investors in your industry will help you better understand the value of your business. I've found these types of meetings beneficial; I learn more about what investors are looking for and what things I can improve in my pitch and my business.

It's always important to remember that there's a cost to bringing on investors. You'll have to structure the proper legal framework for the purchase of equity, set up the rules that govern the organization, and clearly provide the shareholders their rights. Lawyers will have plenty of boilerplate documents to help you do this, but don't think it won't cost you a few precious pennies. Paying too much for legal documents means less growth capital for the business—but it is part of the cost of doing business. Angel Forums cost money to join and so does traveling around pitching to investors. Finally, depending on how or who you raise money with, you may have to pay finder's fee or provide some equity in your company. So, ensure the amount each shareholder invests is worth the legal costs that go alongside it. Check with your lawyer about the legal costs for your financing round and set a minimum amount someone must invest. Don't dilute your equity to pay lawyers.

There's almost nothing more exciting in a start-up than receiving that first big investment. But it'll be all that much sweeter if you don't dilute yourself out of your company in the first eighteen months.

Remember to savor each little success and pat yourself on the back for every milestone. But don't forget it's what you do with that cash that really matters. What you do with it defines your success or failure as an entrepreneur.

Working with Investors

Once you've decided to take on growth capital, you now have a fiduciary and ethical duty to your shareholders. Your shareholders want a founder who will serve the interests of their capital. It seems self-explanatory, I know, but you owe it to them to be transparent, not just about the good things but about the challenges as well. With all the stresses and responsibilities that come with running a company, it's easy to forget about your shareholders. Just remember, they appreciate knowing what's going on—to the extent that is appropriate—for better or worse.

When the company faces tough times financially, and isn't executing on its plan, communication gets the toughest. That doesn't mean you ghost your investors or go dark! You have a shared interest with your shareholders, many of whom have probably "seen it all" when it comes to the struggles of start-ups, and they can be a great resource to discuss these challenges with—so use them!

This is a time when you need to be completely upfront with your current investors, especially if you think they're going to be angry. Hiding bad news might work for a short time, but sooner or later it'll come out, and then you'll have investors not only angry at the bad news, but furious that you weren't transparent. Bad news in business can be recovered from, but the loss of trust will be a permanent injury.

Ultimately, you need to use your best judgment to act in the best interests of the company. Sometimes you need to take drastic action—such as a dilutive financing to "save" the company, or a pivot to an adjacent business model—but this is usually better than the alternative (bankruptcy). If you focus on execution, you can rebuild the lost value over time. If you explain this openly and clearly, most investors will get on board with the idea and support you. Remember, most investors came into this investment understanding the risks, and if you continue to demonstrate integrity and determination, they'll be much more likely to stick with you.

Sometimes an investor may offer some ideas about how to operate your business. When this happens, it's natural to feel a sense of guilt if you don't accept their advice—like you should spend "their" money on their ideas—but remember, if they respected you enough to invest in you and your business, they'll respect you for sticking to your plan. Don't blatantly ignore the opportunity: listen, learn, and assess carefully. But don't let other people's suggestions become a distraction: stay focused and disciplined.

Board Seats

You'll likely be assigning your first board seat along with the first investment you accept. A Board of Directors is comprised of people who collectively supervise the company. In big and/or public companies, they're often elected by the shareholders, but in smaller companies and start-ups either you as founder appoint them or they appoint themselves as a condition of the money they invest.

A board member also carries a fiduciary responsibility in the company, in that they're usually independent of the management and therefore can uphold the company's corporate governance. It's also worth noting, if you've never sat on a board before, that the board has the authority, depending on the shareholders agreement, to remove you, the CEO, if you're failing to perform your duties.

Having directors involved in a company in the early stages can be helpful and important but, as a start-up, you need to ensure your time is spent growing the business and being nimble and efficient in your decision-making. Keep the board seats limited and your meeting times and frequency as minimal as is mandated by your corporate governance. Unless you've taken on millions of dollars' worth of growth capital and have hundreds of shareholders, you don't need seven directors sitting around a table listening to themselves talk and collecting board fees. You do need doers and someone to keep you in check. Nominate directors who understand start-ups, who have industry expertise, and who are willing to step down if it's necessary to accommodate new directors as the business grows and changes.

Ultimately, It's Not About the Money

Money can make people act in destructive, protective, greedy, and anxious ways totally outside their normal character. Even the most professional investors can react with fear when they're scared about losing their investment, and greed when they see an opportunity to make more.

Therefore, the responsibility you carry as the chief executive is to find the best solutions for all—even (and often) in the face of great stresses and uncertainty. You must remain honest and open, but also as unwavering as you can be, so your shareholders will have continued confidence in your character. They may have invested in your company, but at the heart of it they invested in you.

At some point, either your current business idea or a future one will need more money. You want to have a core of investors who know you and trust you, so that you don't have to go through all the pain you endured in your first round of raising capital. There are no guarantees that investors will re-invest with you: maybe your new idea just doesn't appeal to them; maybe their capital is already too heavily deployed; or maybe something has happened in their personal life to limit their investing capacity. Whatever the case may be, don't let your personal character be one of the reasons they don't write you another check.

Your investors will remember what you did, how you did it and who you were as a person while it was being done.

The buck always stops with you.

When it comes to raising money, if you begin with the end in mind, you'll be successful. Be methodical in your process. Have thorough materials that properly outline your company's value potential and exit plan. Raise the right amount of money for the phase of capital you're in. Align with the right people, believe you have a business that is worth investing in, and go for it.

5

Building the Company: Your People

Once you've established your core principles and you've raised some initial funds, you've laid the foundation to build a business. But building your team and establishing a positive company culture are equally critical. Why? Because people, not products, are your most valuable asset.

The People Make the Company

The people who work with you are the lifeblood of the company. Your success is their success and vice versa. Especially in a small company, they're your family outside your family. Company culture matters, because in the early days of a start-up there probably won't be much by way of money, benefits or lucrative stock options to motivate your team. Those early days bring with them a lot of surprises, a lot of setbacks, and no shortage of frustration. To overcome these challenges it's vital that you establish, right from the beginning, a positive company culture. Here are some questions to consider.

- Is the work community you're creating one that your people want to be part of?
- Does this community help people make the type of money they need to survive?
- Do people listen to each other?
- Are they accountable to each other?
- Do they have each other's backs when times get tough?
- Does the community help them grow as individuals beyond their specific roles in the company?

- Will they feel balance in their lives while working with you?
- Will they find a sense of purpose in this community?
- How about feeling safe and free to share their ideas openly?
- Do you celebrate your wins with these people and learn from mistakes?
- Is your place of work one where good ideas win and emotion stays out of the decision-making process?

The establishment of your Core Values and Principles paves the way for a great culture. A great culture, as Peter Drucker says, "eats strategy for breakfast." In other words, outside of having a great product or service, people want community: it may be the next most important thing in building your business. Leading by your own example sets the tone, but hiring the right people brings your culture to life and allows it flourish.

One of the biggest challenges you'll have is hiring the right people. It's important to learn how to assess character in just a few meetings with someone. You can always train people to do a job, especially if they're eager to learn, but you can't train or change someone's true nature.

When talking about our nature, I'm always reminded of a dark, albeit poignant, fable that first appeared in Sanskrit folklore:

One day, a scorpion set out on a journey. He climbed over rocks and under vines and kept going until he reached a river. The river was huge, and the scorpion couldn't see any way across. He ran upriver and then checked downriver, all the while thinking that he might have to turn back.

Then, he saw a frog sitting in the rushes by the bank of the stream on the other side of the river. He decided to ask the frog for help getting across the stream.

"Hellooo, Mr. Frog!" called the scorpion across the water. "Would you be so kind as to give me a ride on your back across the river?"

"Well now, Mr. Scorpion," asked the frog hesitantly, "how do I know that if I help you, you won't try to kill me?"

"Because," the scorpion replied, "if I try to kill you, then I would die too. For you see, I cannot swim!"

Now this seemed to make sense to the frog. But he asked, "What about when I get close to the bank? You could still try to kill me and get back to the shore!"

"This is true," agreed the scorpion, "but then I wouldn't be able to get to the other side of the river!"

"Alright then ... how do I know you won't just wait till we get to the other side and THEN kill me?" said the frog.

"Ahh ..." crooned the scorpion, "because you see, once you've taken me to the other side of this river, I will be so grateful for your help, that it would hardly be fair to reward you with death, now would it?"

So the frog agreed to take the scorpion across the river. He swam over to the bank and settled himself near the mud to pick up his passenger. The scorpion crawled onto the frog's back, his sharp claws prickling into the frog's soft hide, and the frog slid into the river. The muddy water swirled around them, but the frog stayed near the surface so the scorpion would not drown. He kicked strongly through the first half of the stream, his flippers paddling wildly against the current.

Halfway across the river, the frog suddenly felt a sharp sting in his back and, out of the corner of his eye, saw the scorpion remove his stinger from the frog's back. A deadening numbness began to creep into his limbs.

"You fool!" croaked the frog. "Now we shall both die! Why on earth did you do that?"

The scorpion shrugged, and did a little jig on the drowning frog's back.

"I could not help myself. It is my nature."

Then they both sank into the muddy waters of the swiftly flowing river.

Even if you've never run a business before, you've probably known one or two "scorpions" in your life. It's worth watching out for such people. In a business, one bad hire can drag down the morale, faith, and efficiency of an entire start-up.

"Big-Name" Hires

As a rule, avoid hiring people who are way more qualified and demand bigger salaries than where your organization is at that moment, unless you truly have a position they're suited for and they want to be part of where the business is today—not years from now.

Prospective investors often love big hires; they might think Wow, they hired someone who used to run a *50-million-dollar business.* But it's all too easy (and dangerous) to make the mental jump to that *surely means this business will go to 50 million in sales.* It doesn't work that way. These types of experts are much better suited as mentors and directors in the early days of a start-up. The business can't grow to meet the executive.

I made that mistake more than once. In Naked's early days we did manage to secure some pretty big names, and even celebrities, for the team.

To his credit, Alex was never in support of bringing on A-listers at the early stage simply because they often live a different world with expense accounts, fancy hotels, first class flights, and high-touch expectations for the use of their likeness. It's like buying a new car you can't really afford to drive or maintain. I, on the other hand, had always thought it was a great idea to bring on celebrities like they were a silver bullet. It often backfired—sometime worse than others.

This was because I didn't properly manage expectations.

One of my first team members, June, was super-excited with a celebrity we'd brought on. The celebrity—let's call him Jordan—wanted our ads to go on billboards across the country, and June spent an entire week contacting billboard companies and pricing out the campaign. We couldn't afford a billboard campaign—but all that mattered to June was that our star wanted it and so a proposal for a few locations was sent to Jordan for their thoughts. It was all pie-in-the-sky, though, and I never had any intention of doing a billboard campaign. But now June had showed Jordan her proposal, and things came to a head in a pretty acrimonious phone call from Jordan one frosty afternoon.

"I never promised that," I said, gripping the phone to my ear, trying to maintain a civil tone.

"Well your company did!" came Jordan's furious response. "Your team even sent me quotes on bus stop billboards yesterday."

"I don't know why that happened, but Jordan, we're not in a financial position to start buying up billboard ad space all over the country."
"You're not getting sales because you're not getting my image out there. I'm the face of Naked, and without me you're just a punk kid from nowhere!"

Clearly they were upset, and speaking out of frustration … but it stung and was telling, all the same.

"Jordan, I hear you. I really respect what you bring to Naked and I'm trying to give you what you need. But this kind of ad campaign … I thought I told you I need to bring in more investment before we can do this type of campaign."

"Well figure it out, Joel. I've really stuck my neck out for you and I'm not going to be the one hanging if this goes sour. Count on it."

"I understand. Let me talk to the team and see where we're at. I'll let you know soon, okay?"

"Yeah, man. Let's make this happen."

I ended the call and dropped my cell phone on the desk. Knowing I had left the door open (in this case for the possibility of a billboard) instead of giving a firm "no" was a major weakness I had. Maybe that's why June had thought it was okay to send that proposal. Guilt seeped into my veins.

The February sun was streaming in through the bare window but shed little warmth. At least the heating sort of worked here in the office; the warehouse was freezing. I wondered idly if refrigeration would make the boxers last longer.

I rubbed my temples as I tried to think about how to solve the ongoing problems of efficiently distributing product to stores across the country, of maintaining a fresh social media presence, of finding out what that damn smell was in the warehouse, and of scraping together enough cash to pay this month's bills. A fight over billboard ads was the last thing I needed right now!

The silence in the office was deafening. It was so quiet that I could hear every tap of Alex's fingers on his keyboard, over in the other corner. The wind rattled the windows sometimes, so that was something. I didn't know where June was, but at least having her out of the office spared us from another war of words.

It seemed like Alex and June were constantly bickering, and the entire work environment was turning toxic. It didn't help that the Naked board hadn't forgiven me yet for that disastrous decision to make 20,000 pairs of underwear for the original Holt Renfrew order—how long was I going to have to pay for that mistake?—and my more activist investors were keeping a very close eye on operations. With a team as small as Naked's, I couldn't afford to have two key people constantly at each other's throats.

Part of the problem, I realized, was my own lack of leadership. Just like I hadn't put my foot down with June or Jordan and said *no billboards*, to date I hadn't been firm enough with my team about our decision making process. Alex and June might each have contributed to the problem, but it was still my responsibility. I knew what I had to do … I just didn't want to do it.

Either June or Alex had to go—it was clear that they couldn't work together, and I didn't want to bring any new team members into this environment. Jordan was a big fan of June, I knew—probably because June was a big fan of Jordan. But I'd realized over the past few months that June wasn't a great team member. She refused to be led or managed. I'd made some half-hearted attempts to coach her on how to improve but she'd resisted each time.

And then there was Alex.

Turning to look out the window, I recalled not too long ago when our factory had mismatched our thread colors on an exclusive and limited seasonal product run. Although they had agreed to fix the issue, they said it would result in a six-week delay. Dozens of stores across the country had ordered that specific product for this season and the risk of delay would have meant order cancellations en mass. I was upstairs on a sales call and I could hear Alex down below on the mezzanine on his call.

"It's unacceptable," Alex said more sternly than I'd ever heard him speak before. "It doesn't matter if it's a small order. I don't want to hear about your bigger customers. This is your error and your need to be accountable to fixing it first."

A pause followed as he listened

"Wendy," he said, more softly now. "If you're short staffed then I'm coming to your factory with two of my staff to help you and we are not leaving until it is complete. Wendy, I'll literally sleep on your floor for a week until this is fixed."

Another pause.

"Thank you," Alex said even more gently. "We'll be there tomorrow."

Who were we to make such demands, I smirked. No apparel experience, a small company with no established industry credibility. Yet there Alex was, as best he knew how, firing on all cylinders to ensure Naked's success.

He was a machine in his work. He'd completely taken over the operations of the company and freed me to sort out the marketing, sales, and the never-ending search for more investment. No-one else made anywhere near his contribution. Alex was a rare find in his ability to be loyal, a visionary, and a hard worker.

He was exactly the type of partner and team member a start-up needed. My choice over who to keep was pretty obvious.

The big investors had told me to take responsibility and act like a CEO, even if it meant making unpopular decisions. I knew it was the right decision, but still I felt sick with uncertainty. June wasn't a bad person—she just wasn't a good fit for Naked.

I made the decision to let June go. It was an uncomfortable meeting but there were thankfully no fireworks. When she walked silently out the door I hoped that I could close that chapter and move on. But no such luck.

Later that week the phone rang and it was a number I recognized as Jordan. I reached for it, praying that I was wrong and that it was a store manager complaining about bad product instead … that's how badly I did not want to have to take this particular call.

"Hello," I said.

"Joel, you're smart enough to know when you're being a shithead!"

At least angry store managers said hello when they called, I thought.

"You asked me to join this company," Jordan continued, gaining speed, "to be the face, but as soon as you think you've made it you betray me. I still have people asking me where the billboards are."

I tried to respond, but wasn't fast enough as Jordan launched into a furious attack on my character. There was no point trying to fight this tirade, and I realized that I hadn't set a clear expectation from the beginning, so I just put my head down and took it. I picked up a pen and started ticking off the number of times I heard the word "fuck" thrown at me.

Eventually, Jordan seemed to calm down and almost became civil. "You're a good person, Joel, but you've got venom being dripped in your ear, and don't make excuses because that'll just piss me off and I will fuck you over in four minutes. But if you apologize, I'll forgive you because you know I'm that type of person. But one more thing: if you don't fire Alex I will fuck you regardless."

I looked over at Alex, who was by now barking at someone on his own phone. No question, my partner could sometimes rub some people the wrong way in those early days. But I could tell Jordan's words were really the ghost of June speaking … Jordan didn't know Alex enough to care, but June had clearly been talking to him.

"Jordan, you don't really know Alex …"

"I know you had at least one good person on your team, but then you fucked her over and she quit. And it's all because Alex is the only person you listen to, when you actually listen to anyone other than your own ego. Think about it, Joel, and call me in a couple of days."

"I will," I said automatically, again failing to communicate clearly that I'd already made the choice to stick with Alex.

"You better fix things, Joel …"

"I'm running Naked the best way I know how," I said feebly, which resulted in some immediate karma as another tirade began.

"If you do not do this I will see you fucked in the ass so hard you'll feel it for a decade! I will call everyone and I will make sure you never work here again. I will tell them what a slime ball you are and how Naked fucked me. I will make sure you are a nothing even in that little shit town you come from!"

"Jordan …"

"You can rest easy tonight, Joel, because I'm not going to fuck you over tomorrow. But you fire Alex, or your world is over."

The line clicked off.

I was too numb to think. I felt like the dazed boxer about to lose a match, slowly rocking back and forth on my heels as I took shot after shot to the head. I dropped my phone onto the desk and rested my face in my hands.

June, Jordan, angry stores, activist shareholders … it was all my fault. I'd set the wrong expectation with everyone. I should never have brought any celebrities into the company—we just weren't ready. When the squabbling had started internally I should have nipped it in the bud—but I wasn't willing to have the tough conversations early enough and I'd just let it go on and on.

But I'd already made one decision: Alex was staying. Then I made another: I ended our celebrity partnership with Jordan. It was a painful lesson in hiring, managing a team and setting expectations, but the most painful lessons are often the most valuable. In this case, it set Naked on a path toward building a brilliant team.

If ever you have the possibility of bringing a big name onto your start-up team, be wary. This can lead to a single personality dominating the company, whether they try to or not. Bringing in top talent of any kind might sound exciting, but think very carefully about the consequences of doing so.

The big name might bring prestige, but will they actually bring financial gain? Does that celebrity actually have the star power to bring new sales? Is that seasoned business executive actually willing to do his or her own grunt work? Does that high-power talent still have the same reach or abilities when you remove them from their high-power setting and plop them down in a cash-starved, unknown start-up?

Ultimately, as much as shareholders may like big-name executives or stars on the team, they prefer results more. And when you get results, shareholders won't care how you got there.

Team Culture

Talented, loyal employees who take ownership of their job and believe in the greater vision of the company are invaluable to the survival of a business. To truly be a successful team, everyone needs to pull in the same direction. No question: hiring is one of the most challenging parts of starting a business.

I remember one morning in particular, when I dragged my butt into the office after yet another exhausting whirlwind trip to stores on every corner of the continent. Naked had been in full operation for over two years and over the past six months Alex and I had started bringing on more staff members.

Julie was our operations and customer service manager, and she was kind enough to pick me up many mornings (because my car had been condemned and I couldn't afford a new one). On that sunny spring day I saw her parked out in front of my apartment building, saw her waving at me. I waved back and climbed into the car, leaning my head back against the seat and closing my eyes as she pulled away from the curb.

"Did you get that meeting with Barney's in New York?" she asked.

"Yeah, it was positive," I answered. "Not sure about Barney's yet but I dropped in on some other men's stores and we're definitely getting some new orders coming from the trip."

"Awesome—so worthwhile!"

"As always. How are things here?"

She gave me a cheery summary of the events in the Naked office over the past few days, including some sizeable (at least to us) new orders from Holt Renfrew and a new sales agent signed for the southwest region of the US. There were new marketing proposals for me to approve that morning and confirmation had come in that our shipment of computers had officially left Canada and was on its way to Ghana.

The last item actually made me open my eyes. I'd always dreamed of my company being able to make a difference in developing countries, and this was our first big effort—sending computers to a group of schools in Ghana. "Did we get an arrival date?"

"About six weeks," she said, "but it could take easily as long again for them to clear customs and get delivered to the schools."

I had flashbacks to my video camera that had once been held hostage in Peruvian customs. "So no point in me booking my ticket just yet."

"I had a look at prices and there doesn't seem to be much saving in booking early—flying to Ghana is going to be expensive no matter what."

"Yeah. We'll have to look at prices and whether we can afford it."

"Alex says we can't."

"I know," I said with a smile.

We zipped through town, made our usual Starbucks stop, and out to the industrial park where the World Headquarters of Naked Boxer Briefs still hid, sign-less, amongst a motley collection of other small Abbotsford businesses. I pondered, as I so often did, whether we could get a sign made for cheap to put above the door. And then immediately reminded myself, as I always did, that I'd rather pay one of my staff a bit more, or at least take them out for dinner, than buy a sign that no one would ever see. Local branding was an unaffordable luxury for a company where the CEO didn't even own a car and had to bum rides from his staff.

Julie parked and led the way through into the office. Alex was already there, hovering over a computer with the team's latest addition, another accountant named Sandra who was busy learning the company's books in order to free Alex up to take more direct control of operations. His desk was clear, I noted with never-ceasing wonder, with tidy stacks of papers waiting for his review. We'd both grown over the years, but Alex's move to neatness and order was perhaps the most remarkable change.

"Hey Bud," Alex said, straightening. "Welcome home."

I clasped him in a quick hug. "Thanks, man. I didn't even have time to get jet-lagged on this one."

"Do you want to do a meeting this morning? I held off on the regular Thursday meeting in case you wanted to be part of it today."

"Yeah, you bet. Just let me get settled—say, thirty minutes from now?"

"Sounds good."

"I'll tell the team," Julie said.

I walked through into the warehouse, where Husain and Bernadette were stuffing product into packages while they swayed to the beat of Thriller. It was Michael Jackson Friday, courtesy of Alex's love of MJ, and I returned their friendly greetings as I climbed the stairs to the unfinished loft which now served as the sales and marketing workspace.

I was the last to arrive that morning, it seemed. Amber-Lee, our head of sales, was on her phone and no doubt the customer on other end could hear at least some of Thriller. Dan, head of marketing, was focused on his computer. They both greeted me as they were able and I sat myself down at my own desk.

One of the senior buyers at Barney's had emailed, I saw. Her words didn't commit them to anything concrete, but the fact that she'd taken the time to actually write back to me after the meeting spoke volumes. There were other things in my inbox I needed to address, but I'd long ago recognized that on my first day back in the office it was critically important to have face time with each team member.

I was still sipping my coffee when the music faded out and I heard the clunk of people ascending the stairs to the loft. Everybody gathered on chairs and desks in something vaguely resembling a circle, the friendly chatter dying away as Alex began to speak.

"Morning everyone," he said, "thanks for your flexibility in switching the team meeting to today. I know that no-one here responds well to change," there was burst of laughter at that, "but I thought it best for us to meet when Joel was back. Even if he's half-asleep."

"I'm good," I said, hefting my second double espresso.

The meeting unfolded much as every weekly "Rocks" meeting did, with an overall company update from Alex followed by an update from each team member on their area of responsibility. Julie had a positive story about some excellent feedback she'd received via email from customers in California, and Amber-Lee reported that she'd just received a new batch of orders from a few high-end men's clothing stores in Chicago that morning—a success from her own sales trip.

I listened with interest, marvelling at how this team of fun, hardworking young professionals had manifested over the past six months. It was still a weird feeling, hearing someone else tell me what was going on with our little company, but after several false starts I knew, or at least felt certain, that Naked was staffed with bright, trustworthy people who believed in the vision.

When the last of the updates was complete, Alex turned to me. "Any comments, Chief?"

"I don't have an inspirational quote this week," I said as I pulled myself to my feet, "But this week's book prize goes to Julie!" I lifted The Four Agreements by Miguel Ruiz up in the air. "Because not one, not two, but three store accounts reached out to me personally to tell me how amazing you are when they call and complain about needing another week to pay their bills."

Everyone laughed again. Each week we tried to acknowledge a different staff member who had gone above and beyond by giving them a book.

"But seriously, I did have the chance to meet with Barney's and a few boutiques while in New York and I really think we've caught their attention—not just with our product, but with our culture. I raved about you guys and all the tremendous work you put in, every day here at Naked. We have a great product, but more than that we have great people." I gestured at Julie again and then I nodded to Amber-Lee. "Because of your efforts we've increased our footprint in Chicago." And then over to Dan, "And you convinced The Bay to give us that pop-up shop for their Men's Week!" I put down my espresso to gesture with both hands, feeling the positive vibe that I so loved about this place.

"Every aspect of what we do matters, from sourcing the right materials to shipping without error to ensuring our money is spent wisely and well. I've always said that Naked is more than just a product, more than just a company. It's a way of being. It's about being comfortable in your own skin, being confident in yourself and having fun on your own terms."

They'd heard it all before and were good enough to indulge my brand tangents and tendency to use platitudes a little excessively. I cast my gaze across the whole team, realizing suddenly just how much I'd come to care about them like family.

"It's about being true to yourself. It's about getting naked." I smirked a little, realizing how ridiculous it would have sounded to anyone who accidently walked in at that very moment. But I held onto the moment in hopes of ending on at least a semi-serious tone.

Dan was the closest person, and I placed a hand on his shoulder. "You guys make this company what it is, and I always enjoy coming home." I smiled. "Now get those MJ tunes cranked and get back at it!"

A mixture of cheers and laughter rose from the team, and Alex herded them on their way.

I remember this day in particular because, not only was it one of those truly ideal days where you just feel so good about your team but also right after that meeting, Alex told me in no uncertain terms that Naked couldn't afford to fly me to Ghana to present the computers to the schools. I wasn't happy—I'd really been looking forward to that trip, and to the positive exposure it would bring for the company—but I didn't argue. He was right, of course, and he was keeping the best interests of Naked at the forefront.

I was annoyed, though, because this project had taken two years to put together and I desperately wanted to be part of the celebrations there (and selfishly have a bit of travel adventure to a far off new country again). After, admittedly, testily agreeing with him I stepped away to gaze out across the warehouse. Michael Jackson was still blaring, and I could see that Julie had joined Husain and Bernadette in getting product ready for shipping. It was only Bernadette's job specifically to pack the orders, but everyone helped out if needed. Naked didn't pay them much more than the lowest the industry would bear, but here they were, having fun while they worked hard for a company they believed in.

Maybe the whole world wouldn't know about the schools in Ghana, but we would! And that realization, that I'd built something special right here at home in this amazing team, brushed away any disappointment or fatigue I might have felt. I smiled to myself as I looked around at the rest of my hardworking team. Everybody got it: everybody here got Naked.

Hiring Smart

Assembling this team didn't just happen. The process of building it began right at the job description, posting and interview process. Alex and I were always upfront with potential hires—we wanted them to know exactly what they were walking into and what was expected of them. The idea of working a start-up can often sound better than it actually is. Likewise, we were very careful to tease out what our potential hires wanted to do most, and then figure out if that matched our requirements.

Let's say you post a job for a marketing position that's primarily focused on customer service, with a bit of social media work as a minor task. Your potential hire might think, "Sure I'll do some customer service," while dreaming of working on your Instagram account all day. After a week or two of doing mostly customer service and no Instagram, they may become disgruntled and go find another job where they can do exactly what they want. This wastes your time and theirs—best to ensure expectations are aligned before you ever sign them up.

When interviewing potential team members, ask questions like:

"What is your superpower?"

"What was your favorite past project you worked on?"

By asking these questions, you'll know what they truly want to do. If you can't offer them enough of their "superpower" type work, then they may not be a fit for your company right now.

Also, have a casual conversation to determine if they're a good culture fit. Just "getting to know them" through small talk can go a long away in assessing how someone may fit in with your team.

Then, if the situation is suitable, give them a small paid project to test their work.

Remember too that in start-ups team members often have to wear many different hats (also known as doing a variety of tasks), only a few of which they actually want to wear. Adaptability and a certain comfort with improvisation and uncertainty are essential for start-up team members.

Chip Wilson, the amazingly successful founder of Lulu Lemon did this almost better than any by having his team members take the personal and professional Landmark Forum methodology. Doing this provided Lulu Lemon team members an awareness of the way people (including themselves) think and act, providing the tools and common language for effective internal communication. If you didn't like the Landmark Forum you probably shouldn't have been working at Lulu Lemon, thus leaving a company with very likeminded people. Yes, sometimes as specific as requesting someone take the Landmark Forum can be tough to do with a large company and sometimes the downside is an almost "cultish" feeling in the workplace, but at least in those early days everyone is rowing in the same direction!

Lastly, if you hire a new team member and they do their job poorly early on, ask yourself: "Is this because of how we've trained them or supported them? Are they in the wrong position or do they simply not know how to do the job adequately?"

Consider whether you've given them proper feedback. As children we're taught to be nice. You know the expression, "if you don't have anything nice to say, don't say anything at all." Well, that doesn't exactly work when building a business (or in life for that matter). If you don't say something because you think it's not nice or it may hurt someone's feelings, you're actually hurting yourself and that team member.

I prefer: "Is it kind, necessary, or true?" Critical feedback for a team member may not seem kind (even though it actually is) but it's certainly necessary and true. Why? Because if they aren't doing their job right and you don't tell them and give them a chance to improve, then when you fire them you actually have failed them. Feedback is critical!

You're equally responsible for your team member's success. If you've hired incorrectly, either move them to a different task or let them go with fair compensation, because it's not good for them or the company to be stuck in a place where they're not succeeding.

If you're unable to find, or can't afford, the right employees, you can always hire contractors for the short term. You can often test potential employees with a small paid contract project before hiring them. This will allow you to determine if their skill set aligns with what you need, and whether they have the right personality fit for your culture. Contracts can be excellent in helping your business grow without the financial commitment of an employee, but there are a few very important things to remember when hiring contractors.

Contractors aren't always team players and don't always fit the company's culture. Often they've gained their experience in the corporate environment and left because they're independent in nature—that's why they work for themselves. They'll have their own operating principles and processes and will want very clear objectives for the scope of their work and conditions for success.

Ultimately, you can't build a culture or team around a contractor, because you're not their boss—they are. Using contractors can be a good employment option when you're just getting started—when cash is low, workload is inconsistent and you're "trying team members on for size"—but eventually you're going to have to commit to team members, especially if you expect them to commit to your company.

When I first started Naked, I had to do almost everything myself—simply because I was the only person on the team. When Alex joined we worked as partners, communicating constantly and sharing tasks as the moment required. We each had our superpowers, but we could also step into the other's role at a moment's notice. This sort of symbiotic work style can be effective when you're just getting started, but as soon as you start to bring on actual staff members, you need to start to define roles more clearly.

When you're hiring you need to separate yourself from the "I must do everything myself" mindset. Surround yourself with people who are more talented and specialized than you at their specific task. Surround yourself, as Apple does, with people who tell you what to do! If you're personally in the weeds of your business for too long, relied on for every decision, you can't scale your business.

Don't ask yourself, "How can I do this?" Instead ask, "Who can do this?" Hiring right also allows your company to scale up.

Ensure the amazing people you surround yourself with are also not individualists. Have people work together to contribute to the problem-solving and keep people aware of all the Projects, Goals, Rocks, and Objectives the company has going on. If your team members don't connect the dots between projects themselves, make the connections for them—unite them.

In my experience, if your team's salary and job security requirements are met, the things that most motivate team members are contribution, connection, and personal growth. They might be pleased to hear that the company has hit its financial goals for the year, but they won't get charged up by this. As CEO your goals might be really tied up with the company's financial success, but unless you make your team members shareholders they'll be motivated by other things. Find out what those things are. What about their personal goals? What role are you and the company playing in helping them achieve their goals? Ensure you're taking care of your team members' well-being and don't make assumptions about it— ask, and aim to understand them.

Building a solid team culture can have other, unexpected benefits as well. I remember a time when my friend (and former) boss, Cam, mentioned that he'd like to stop by the Naked office on Friday afternoon. Cam and I had gone to the same high school, although I'd hesitate to say we "went to high school together" because he was four years older than me and in my eyes he was just one of those cool, popular seniors than everyone wanted to be friends with. He at least knew my name through our mutual sporting activities, but we didn't really get to know each other until, five years later, we headed to Thailand for six months as part of the same group of four guys.

You can't help but be transformed in some way by living overseas together for half a year, and when we came home Cam and I were close friends. He went on to start a company that painted lines on roads, and he even gave me a job when I was broke and desperate.

A few months before that particular Friday afternoon, I'd approached Cam about investing in Naked. Like always, he took his time to answer, and I suspected this visit to the Naked offices was to discuss the subject.

Cam was one of those people who seemed to know everyone. This included Julie, so when he arrived at the office he received a greeting almost as if he worked there.

Hearing him say hello to the team downstairs, I realized I was actually nervous. You'd think two guys who'd spent six months in Thailand together would be beyond feeling nervous, and my own reaction was surprising. Even when he was my boss I never felt nervous around him, and that included the time when I accidentally left a minor swerve in a permanent thermoplastic white line on the road (let's just say line painting wasn't exactly my true calling). But today, with much-needed capital on offer the stakes felt high. And more than that, I realized, Cam was still a bit of a hero in my eyes, with a successful business, and today I was showing him my own corporate creation. His opinion mattered to me.

He came upstairs with Alex and we all sat at the boardroom table. It made things look very fancy, but in fact we'd got it for free from an office-closing clearance event—never say no to free furniture!

The three of us chatted about sports, how his business was doing, some of the business trips I'd been on recently, until we finally got to where we all knew the conversation was going.

"How is Naked doing?" Cam asked.

All things considered, it was doing well and growing so Alex and I took him through the ins and outs of our successes and challenges. We were expanding our store presence across the continent and new products were being developed. Alex ran him through the numbers and how much capital investment we needed to get to our next milestone.

And then, knowing full well the challenges of finding and keeping good people in a company, Cam asked, "And the team ... how are they?"

This was easy. They were incredible. But how did I convey this in a way that didn't just make him think I was feeding him positive news? Then I remembered something he and I had gone through back in Thailand.

"Let me put it this way," I said. "Remember when we were at the full moon party in Ko Pha Ngan with our crew?"

Cam gave me a knowing nod and look of *Buddy, how I could ever forget?*

"Well, remember how I took off and forgot to tell you guys I'd left?"

"Yep," Cam replied with deadpan humor. "I was turning over bodies all morning looking for you!"

"What?" Alex asked, jaw dropping.

"We're at this beach party," Cam explained, settling back in his chair. "Hundreds of people, all of them drunk. We four are all doing our own thing, and I haven't seen Joel in an hour so I assume he's getting lucky somewhere at this bar."

"I wish," I added. "Around two am I just staggered off back to our hostel—but in my drunkenness I didn't think to tell any of the other three guys."

"So at sunrise when he hadn't returned," Cam said, "we're looking around and can't find Joel anywhere. You gotta understand that there were about a hundred people sleeping or passed out on the beach, and I figured Joel was one of them. So I started rolling over bodies to look for him."

"You were rolling over bodies?" Alex echoed in amazement.

"Yep," I interjected. "The other two guys gave up and went to bed— remember, they'd been up all night, too—but Cam by now was sure that I was passed out in the sand, and there was no way he was leaving me for the crabs."

Cam laughed. "So imagine, Alex, how pissed I was when I'd turned over about a hundred bodies, then dragged my ass back to the hostel, only to find this little shit passed out in the door to our room!"

"But the point is," I said with emphasis, "the other guys bailed, and left me to my fate. Cam stayed on the beach and searched every single body to make sure I wasn't left behind. That is true friendship."

Cam nodded modestly.

"And ..." I paused for dramatic effect, "the type of people we have here at Naked would all have stayed behind to roll over bodies."

Cam let out a bit of laugh. But in his eyes, I could see that he understood.

'Okay, Joel," he said, "where do I sign?"

And with that, Cam wrote the company a cheque for much-needed investment. Because we were friends, maybe. Because the company showed promise, probably. But it was our team that convinced him the most. He knew that with a great team, anything is possible.

Your team will evolve and grow as your company does, and try your best to plan ahead for big changes. When your company finally crosses the chasm, so to speak—raises a significant amount of growth capital, goes through a merger or is acquired by a larger company—you'll likely start to bring on new team members with big fancy resumes.

It's critical, in my opinion, that the integral first team members find roles in the company past these events. Although they may not have the pedigree on their resume and their early contributions may have been greater because of their willingness and eagerness to be helpful across all facets of the company, you still want these people here! You should give them every opportunity to have success with you. They went through the initial hellfire, they have valuable institutional knowledge of your business, your customers, and your "Why". Find ways to mentor and train these loyal team members so they can grow as your organization grows. You owe them that.

6

Products, Customers and Marketing

I want to share a few words on processes, product development, customers, and marketing. Given the magnitude of these topics, you're probably thinking: why just a few words?

Every business is unique. Its products, customers and markets may be completely different from all others. How we market and sell to our customers is ever changing and evolving. When I first started Naked, the idea of running an ecommerce-only business saw me laughed out of many rooms. Instagram and YouTube stars and micro influencers didn't really exist. We all know what's happened since then—what's next?

That's why I only want to focus on a few tried and true principles that I believe will help guide you as you build out your individual plan.

Process and Product Development

Whether the product you're developing is going to cost $0.10 or $10,000 to make, it's critical to be process-driven and to know whether or not you have a market for what you're making at the price you want to sell it. Even when you're just starting out!

To do this well, you need to have a good, consistent, reliable and well-understood process in place. Your process, with checks and balances, will help minimize errors and inefficiencies that cost you time and money. Good product development is about way more than just effort.

Keep in mind that when you're trying to build innovative products, you're *frequently* going to have ideas or prototypes that fail. But these failures should come from experimentation and testing, not from errors in your company's process.

Determining whether you have a market for your product comes down to research, feedback, and product testing. Sure, you may see a need for your product. Sure, you may have developed some samples that your family and friends say they like. But does the world really want, at this specific moment in time, what you're offering? A good product development process will help you answer these questions.

Let me tell you about a time, early in Naked's history, where we *didn't* follow this process.

After our pair of maulings on Dragons' Den, Naked had gained enough national exposure that we'd secured our first big investors and we'd started to sell into small boutique stores across Canada. We still didn't have any orders from national stores, but I'd been pitching hard. Those efforts finally led to a fateful afternoon in the small Naked office where Alex and I, the only employees of the company at the time, worked.

"Hey Joel," he exclaimed, hurrying over. "Did you see the email from Holt Renfrew?"

Holt Renfrew. I'd been stalking their underwear buyer for months, and finally secured a phone meeting. The buyer had seemed perplexed for the first few minutes of the call as to how I'd gotten her number in the first place, and I'd struggled to get through to her what my product actually was. Sensing enough interest, I told a little fib, saying that I'd be in Toronto and that I wanted to show her my product line while there. I was planning on going to Toronto, but only if she, and a few others, accepted my request for a meeting. Which she did, and since she couldn't wear the product herself, I brought underwear for her boyfriend or fiancé, her dad, and male colleagues ... I wanted everyone in her circle to tell her they loved it.

But since the meeting it had been radio silence for weeks.

"No, what'd it say?" I asked, intrigued by the clear excitement on Alex's face.

"They're in! The initial order is for nine hundred pairs for November, in six doors across Canada. They say that their top brands tend to sell-through a thousand pairs a month, so we'll need to be ready for re-orders."

I stared at Alex for a long moment. I heard the words, but somehow they didn't make sense. It didn't sound like a rejection ...

"Holy shit!" I said with sudden realization. "That's awesome!"

"I know. Here's the thing, though. They want white product as well as black."

"We don't have any white fabric."

"Yeah, but that's what they want."

My mind was racing. The most influential fashion store in Canada had bought Naked underwear! And if they wanted white as well as black, we'd make it happen. I wasn't sure how much money was still left in the pot, but two of our big investors had been making noises lately about wanting to invest more.

"If you want to do this we'll need to air ship white fabric from Italy," Alex said, already thinking through the practicalities. "And we'll have to order a rush job at the factory. Not only will that erode our entire margin but I'm not sure we have enough cash to cover that."

I clapped his shoulder and led him toward the office. "I got an idea.

Don't worry, man: some way or another, we are going to make this happen."

"I think we should plan on making four thousand pairs; that'll give us some inventory for re-supply."

It was a sensible suggestion. Making extras would reduce our cost-per-unit and give us ready inventory in case the first batch sold through quickly. But unlike Alex (who was always practical), I was a dreamer and with this great news I was dreaming big. So I made a fateful decision.

"No, we'll burn through that way too fast. Think of the marketing initiatives we already have planned. We're going to produce twenty thousand."

Naked was, in my opinion, unstoppable.

Alex spun to face me. "You're joking, right?"

"We have to think big," I said with an excited grin. "It's way better to have some extra product in our warehouse for a month or two than run out and have nothing to sell—especially right before Christmas."

"But the initial order is just shy of a thousand. Twenty thousand is complete overkill and undisciplined."

After years of trying to get my dream off the ground, I was tired of naysayers, and tired of being pushed around.

"Twenty thousand," I said firmly. "That's my decision. And we're going to get right back on the phone to The Bay and to all the indie stores. If Holt's on board they're all going to want to be too."

"But how are we going to afford that?" Alex's voice was rising dangerously.

I gave him a confident smile. "I'll talk to the investors. They're going to love this."

The dream was coming true.

Or so I thought. We burned all our cash and maxed our credit to rush through orders for twenty thousand pairs of Naked underwear—half of them in a color we'd never done before—on an insane deadline to get them boxed and in stores by September. It was a titanic achievement of which I was very proud, and completely ignorant of just how crazy it actually was. Naked was in the top stores in Canada, and we had a warehouse full of inventory ready to restock as our product flew off the shelves.

Except Naked didn't fly off the shelves. Oh, it sold okay, but not in the numbers I'd dreamed it would. The nineteen thousand pairs in inventory pretty much just sat, with occasional, small re-orders coming in and making another small empty space in the otherwise-full warehouse.

And then customer reviews started coming in. Some people loved the boxers, but there was also a pretty consistent complaint about how they didn't stay up. Guys were finding they had to constantly pull up their underwear during the day, and they were pretty annoyed about it. One guy even said, "Now I know why you call it Naked … because it doesn't stay on!"

We investigated the problem and realized that our design only fit slim guys really well. Anyone with a thicker frame or a gut was having this problem of the boxers sliding off. We realized that it was a design flaw. A fixable one, but it would mean creating a whole new batch on inventory and recalling the old design.

As I stared at the nineteen thousand pairs of now unsellable product sitting in my warehouse, I learned the lesson of the importance of establishing a process in product development.

Over the years, I've seen too many entrepreneurs spend money to make a huge number of their product because a buddy or a parent said they really liked the idea, but without having any clue how they were going to sell it, or even if anyone really wanted or needed it. My 20,000-unit first order nightmare was a case in point. Other than a couple of purchase orders from stores, I really had no idea if the end customer would vote, with their dollars, on the price of the garment, the colors we'd selected or even connect with our messaging or the idea of "Feeling Like You're Wearing Nothing at All" in your underwear.

Our initial market research suggested they would, and my dad and a few friends liked the underwear, but we had no customer proof and no downside protection in case the product didn't sell.

So ... lesson learned. A lesson so expensive and so damaging to our reputation that we nearly went under in our first year of full operations.

But we learned. And Naked adopted a research-based design philosophy that served us well as we rolled out new designs for boxer briefs, T-shirts, and other companion products. It worked well and I carried it on to my follow-on businesses.
Here's how we do it now:

1. We establish focus groups within our customer or potential customer base to see what it is that they want and need in products. What can't they find out there?

2. We conduct SEO research to see if people are in fact searching for those products. If people are searching for products it usually means that A) they're interested in that type of product, and B) they're uncertain about some aspect of what they want to buy and are doing research, and C) they don't have a specific brand they're immediately going to for the purchase.

3. We select a product we want to make and conduct a competitive analysis on that product in order to determine our retail price targets, unique features and benefits, and whether our focus groups have missed something.

4. Based on this research, we then design a series of products that are in line with our brand image and design ethos.

5. Once our designs are rendered and colors selected, we survey our customers and invite them to vote on which styles, price points, colors and features they're most likely to buy. Essentially, our own customers are helping us merchandise our collection. This is critical because, as designers, we often love a little too much of what we design, and it's incredibly hard to edit things out.

6. Finally, we'll produce samples of the product and aim to pre-sell it on crowdfunding platforms such as Kickstarter or Indiegogo. We also pre-sell on our website.

7. Once we hit a minimum sales target we go into production on that item. If we don't hit the minimum target, we won't produce the goods.

Of course, I'm talking about a process that's designed for apparel and consumer goods—it'll be different for other industries. But the principle remains the same—take out as much guesswork as possible, as early as possible.

Research-based design isn't foolproof. It can be misleading because the potential customer hasn't yet had to actually hand over their hard-earned dollar, and you still have to execute on the product they want. That said, it certainly reduces the risk for start-ups using too much cash on products they're not completely sure will sell.

Research-based design should definitely incorporate your own inspirations or brand vision. But it adds to that by, in the early days, using feedback to guide development of those ideas. Longer term, once you have sufficient data about what your customers like and a loyal customer base to sell your products to, you can drop certain aspects of this model, such as the pre-sales on Kickstarter. It's up to you and your business model, but keeping close tabs on what your customer wants and needs as part of your product development is critical to your relevancy and ongoing success.

A story about protecting your downside come from one of the most iconic entrepreneurs in the world—Sir Richard Branson. As the story goes, Branson was upset because of a canceled American Airlines flight to the British Virgin Islands. So he hired a private plane, made a sign that read "Virgin Airlines one-way $39 to the British Virgin Islands" and managed to fill his flight with everyone else whose flight had also been canceled.

The next day he called up Boeing, leased a plane and started Virgin Airlines.

Now, of course at this point Branson was already financially successful with his Virgin Records store and had the ability to take this gamble. However, Sir Richard protected his downside by convincing Boeing to only lease him an aircraft. This way he didn't have to buy the multi-million-dollar asset that he'd be stuck with if Virgin Airlines didn't work.

Go ahead and be bold in jumping into ideas, but protect your downside through research, clear and defined development processes, and product testing where no degree of scrutinizing is too much!

Product Market Fit

Another key to success is determining whether you have product market fit before you produce anything in high quantities. The Product Market Fit (PMF) concept was developed and named by

Andy Rachleff. It's also referred to as Minimum Viable Product.

Essentially, what PMF means is that you've satisfied a strong market demand for your product. You can tell you have it if word of mouth is spreading about your product, positive media reviews are coming in, and, most importantly, customers are buying it as fast they can.

Andy Rachleff simplifies it even further: "If the customer doesn't scream, you don't have Product Market Fit because if they're not going to buy it at the end of 30 days, they're not desperate, and if they're not desperate, you don't have Product Market Fit."

If these things aren't happening and you keep having to spend lots of money to generate sales, you probably haven't hit the mark with your idea and you should go back to the drawing board or abandon that product entirely.

If you've found Product Market Fit you should be able to scale quickly, even profitability, based on that product.

You certainly don't need to be the first product to market to achieve PMF: you just need to be the first product that finds a true market fit—and you should make that product better than the rest of your direct competitors. I mentioned earlier that Google was the eighteenth search engine to launch. Can you think of seventeen other search engines now (or remember those from back in 1998)?

To give you an example of the glaring difference between having and not having PMF, here's an example from my second start up (Kickstarter wasn't around when I launched Naked). We were making clothing and gear that targeted Millennial world travelers. Our first product, a travel bag for men and women, did well on Kickstarter and achieved nearly $100,000 in sales in thirty days. At the time $100,000 in sales put us in the top 1% of all Kickstarter campaigns. Pretty good, right?
We weren't convinced, though … Although we'd achieved a decent amount of sales it didn't really seem like people were "screaming" for

our product and our return on ad spend was just barely profitable. It's worth noting we hadn't used our research-by-design process for this bag.

Fast forward one year and, using our research-based design process, we launched a functional yet stylish travel dress on Kickstarter. This campaign produced nearly $1,000,000 in sales in thirty-five days, becoming one of the most successful apparel campaigns of all time. The campaign hit a high of 27:1 return on ad spend (which means for every 1 dollar we spent on ads we returned 27 in gross sales). Following the campaign, we averaged about $10,000 per month in completely organic ecommerce sales on our own website.

That was Product Market Fit. Instead of making bags ... we pivoted our focus to dresses.

Lastly, think about the product's longevity. Is it timeless and built to last? Is it recession-proof? Is there planned obsolescence or is this product being designed for a trend that may not last? How fast can you build, produce, or iterate your product and how important is speed-to-market? Maybe speed-to-market isn't important, but building barriers to entry (i.e. making it hard or impossible for new competitors to enter your specific market niche) is.

Ultimately, your customer will decide. But if you've done your research, built the best product to match their needs, and have in place solid, adaptable processes, you have the best chance to either succeed or at least fail with minimal costs.

Customers

Your business—product or service—is oxygen to your customer and they're oxygen to you. In other words, you need each other, in an exchange of value. If your customers don't need you, then, I'm sorry to say, you don't have a business. A customer isn't just a number on a spreadsheet, money in your till, or a name on a packing label.

They're human beings who are trying to thrive, understand and express themselves. Your product or service helps them do that and, in turn, their loyalty and hard-earned dollars help you continue to create and build your business.

So treat them as such. Treat them as human beings. How you choose to interact with your customers and partners will be driven by your Principles and Core Values and how well you do it will come down to the people on your team.

Human beings crave connection. First, they'll make their decision on whether to buy your products based on the merits of the product itself and how it fits into their store, wardrobe, or life. However, once you establish a connection with them, their purchasing decision becomes an emotional one. No longer do they only purchase from you because of what the product or service provides for them, but also because of how it, or you (the company), makes them feel.

Build it into your budget to visit the owners, sales managers, and buyers of the stores carrying your product. Don't forget the sales associates. When you meet these people, make eye contact, and smile! Being with people, enjoying small talk and showing that you're listening goes a long way in establishing trust. Really listen, in order to hear and understand their hopes and struggles.

In online Direct to Consumer businesses, you'll have to find ways of doing this via email, ACTUAL MAIL, or messenger services like Zen Desk. Where possible, the phone is better! We once hired an aspiring sales associate to call our customers directly and ask what they liked and didn't like about our products and if there was any way we could make their experience better. It went very well— most people were pretty shocked that we called them and were not trying to sell them anything. Ask yourself how you can go above and beyond to make the customer experience memorable. Show them that you care about them and are grateful for their patronage.
Connection leads to trust. Trust leads to long-term relationships. Depending on your business, it may cost you a fair bit of time and

money to build trust, but it'll pay dividends in the long run.

When it comes to your customers, sometimes things just don't work out for them … which means, things don't work out for you. Maybe a customer doesn't like a product, or it shows up damaged, or it just doesn't sell in the first place. If you've been honest and done everything you could to create a positive interaction or result, many people will place value on that.

This is called "service recovery" in MBA circles. Every company, no matter how well it's run or how good its product, sometimes makes a mistake. When (not if) this happens to you, respond quickly to make it right.

First, embrace the error. Don't try to ignore it or dismiss it.

Second, find out as quickly as possible what went wrong. If it was a failure by your company or your distribution team, take responsibility for it. If it was a failure by the customer, explain to them their error without judgement or accusation. It's amazing how much a friendly and open attitude by your company can defuse a customer's anger. Alternatively, an evasive or confrontational attitude by your company can easily escalate a customer's ire.

Third, fix the problem. Whatever the problem is, you will have the power to make it right for the customer somehow. Even if you can't undo the error (perhaps your delivery arrived too late for your customer to make use of it, and the moment is lost) you can certainly offer some sort of compensation to ease the sting. This may be as simple as refunding their money, but ideally it's something that can help to build an ongoing relationship. Maybe you can offer them an exclusive pre-launch wear test on an upcoming new product, or maybe you can send a replacement product with a gift card. If you're not sure how to make it right for the customer, ask them. Even the fact that you included them in the direction of the service recovery will go a long way to rebuilding the relationship.

Your actions express what matters to you—make sure your customers matter!

Treating people fairly is the right thing to do. And you should "fire" customers who don't treat you and your team right as well. Toxic customers are akin to toxic employees. They drag down the morale of your team, cause issues, don't pay bills, post bad reviews wherever they can (Yelp, Facebook, Amazon, your website), and set the standard for how you allow yourself and your team to be treated.

Ultimately, it's impossible to make everyone happy; but do everything you can to build connections and have positive interactions.

In our digital age, sales have changed dramatically from when I started Naked. But even so, I'm going to share a story about how making this extra effort saved Naked.

Remember the 20,000-unit nightmare? At that time we probably sold our products in thirty stores across Canada—stores that certainly had customers who would be wearing our "non-fitting" sizes. Naked had various independent sales agents across the country who sold to most of these accounts, so I hadn't actually met the store buyers personally.

But with this crisis, it was time to get on the phone … which I did. But instead of just doing a phone call and offering an exchange or refund, I told them I'd visit them personally to apologize and bring the updated products for their review. So, in the dead of a Canadian winter, in a car that was eventually condemned, I drove thousands of kilometers, as well as hopped on a few flights, to visit each and every one of our stores. Despite some fairly harsh customer complaints, they all gave us another shot.

Naked could have been sunk in its first year by our design flaw and my bad decision to make 20,000 pairs. But I owned both errors and went to great lengths to try and fix it for our stores. They noticed, and they were impressed. And my company stayed in business.

Ever since then, I've made a point of visiting almost every store, factory, or supplier that I've ever worked with. The personal connection really makes a difference.

Simply put, both product market fit and customer service come down to effort. Both require an extra step that takes time to ensure that A) you're targeting the right people with the right product and B) you're taking care of those people.

Marketing

Previously we talked about your business purpose, your "Why"— your reason for being. This is the genesis of marketing. The specifics of how you market are, much like product development, unique to your business. There are, however, two key principles I believe you must always keep in mind.

The first is what I consider the holy grail of timeless marketing rules and it comes from market legend Seth Godin in his book *All Marketers Are Liars*, a book about the importance of telling an authentic story and ensuring that story is built into your product.

What caught me most about his book is a motto that I always come back to: "Don't try to change someone's worldview."

In other words, don't try to convince people who don't associate with your brand, values, beliefs, product, or story, to do so. It's a fool's errand, and often a very expensive one. Another way of putting this is: don't try to please everyone.

The "please everyone" segment of the market is impossible to win and is over-crowded with competition. Instead, find a niche and give them exactly what their worldview wants in terms of a brand story and product story.

These early adopters of your product, the ones that share your world view, can be called your tribe or your true fans.

Choose your target market

When I was graduating from high school my mother took me on a special date to the "Big City" to buy a suit. Having worn hand-me-downs my entire my life, the prospect of a new suit and a day in the city had me bursting with excitement. On the big day my mother and I headed to downtown Vancouver to a store called Holt Renfrew—yes, the same Holt Renfrew of the 20,000-unit disaster—the nicest luxury clothing store in Canada. Walking across the glass corridor from Pacific Center mall into Holt Renfrew, my jaw hit the floor. Oh … the style and class of the place. I'd never seen clothes that looked so good!

My mom then said to me, "Joel, this is your grandma's favorite store, it's my favorite store and one day, when you make a lot of money, you'll be able to shop here …"

And then we crossed the street to a cheap suit store and I bought my discounted grad suit—a few sizes too big in case I might still grow into it, of course. (For the record … I never did!)

My mom only meant to inspire, and she did create a lasting impression because Holt Renfrew became the store I needed to put Naked underwear into when we launched. I'm proud to say it was our first big store and when I trained their team, I shared that very story. But my point here is only that Holt Renfrew created a clear brand and were always consistent with it. They were high-end, high-quality, and they never compromised. They made a decision to go after a certain sector of the market and they didn't try to please everyone. They weren't trying to get my business when I was a dirt-poor high school kid!

At Naked when we first launched, the idea of a brand called "Naked" was offensive or too risqué to a fair amount of people. That really didn't matter because we weren't trying to please everyone. In fact, it can be a good thing if some people get a little offended by your brand or product. Think about Patagonia's strong activism for the environment. Do you think some people might be put off when they call out a certain President of the United States about his track record on National Parks and the climate crisis? Heck yes, but that only makes their true fans love them more. If they tried to speak to everyone, they'd ultimately speak to no-one at all.

A small group of true fans doesn't have to mean a small business. Once something has been validated by true fans, others follow. A great example of this is how apparel giant Lulu Lemon built their global powerhouse brand around Yoga instructors, practitioners, and those who cared about wellness. Eventually, as wellness expanded into a mainstream idea practiced by millions, Lulu grew to become a four billion dollar company.

Had Lulu Lemon initially tried to also cater their brand (and their black stretchy pants—their claim to fame) to hockey players, footballers, and the entire sports world, their core fans wouldn't have felt so "tribal" or "passionate" about the product and what the company was trying to stand for.

Always be consistent

This leads to my second key marketing principle: Discipline and Consistency.

These may be the two least sexy words about marketing but they're also the most important—for all companies, but especially for start-ups.

Be consistent with your company and product story. Be consistent in creating marketing content for your core market (those that share your world view). This is always easier said than done.

In start-up land you'll have five options for every dollar you can spend. On the surface, every idea will sound like a good one that's going to get you sales and make your product famous. Understand that those glorious hopes almost never come true. Besides, hope is not strategy … I know I've made that mistake!

As Naked began to enjoy some success in Canada, Alex and I turned our sights toward the vast American market. If the company was going to be a success, we knew we had to build our brand and gain a retail presence in our giant neighbor to the south. After what must have been a dozen trips to Seattle (some invited, others not), a night of line dancing in Dallas, and a few times detained at the US border crossing, the retail icon Nordstrom had given us an order. But expanding our marketing and distribution needed more money and it seemed like we were burning through cash faster than we could raise it, with the hope of the big breakthrough in sales always "just around the corner". Sure, the company revenues were growing, but the marketing machine was voracious and we just couldn't shovel cash into its maw fast enough.

We'd basically tapped out all the investors in our hometown of Vancouver, and we'd learned from the Jordan experience to resist the lure of Los Angeles and Hollywood talent. Alex suggested we work the wealthy apparel communities of Toronto and Montreal, two big Canadian cities we knew fairly well—but I was, as usual, thinking bigger. The epicenter of North American fashion was New York, and I was convinced that if we could land some big New York investors, all roads would lead to gold.

Pretty soon I was travelling to New York every month, meeting with wealthy investors and fashion bigwigs as I pitched and pitched and pitched the vision of Naked. Most of the time Alex stayed behind in Abbotsford, running the operations and managing our awesome team while I kept up a near-constant cycle of personally visiting all our stores and meeting New York luminaries. The exposure was great, but everyone in New York had an opinion—and most of those opinions were telling me to do something different with my company. Go down market and sell underwear cheap; go up market and be more premium; focus on the women's line; focus on the gay community; expand; simplify; make it more sexy; make it more minimalist. Even the bankers I was meeting had opinions about what deal structures I should be presenting, whether I should take debt or sell equity, what valuation I should be asking … I was being pulled in every direction by people who knew a lot more about the fashion industry than I did. But, I realize now, nobody knew Naked like I did.

Our marketing and business development consistency suffered a lot in those years as I tried to listen to advice from all over; and I'm convinced to this day that this lack of discipline hurt our growth as we tried, ultimately, to be too many things and failed to be loyal to what we really were. Adding to this, the team's core was slowly upset by the instability created through my focus on New York and all that was happening there for Naked.

As a start-up you rarely have the opportunity to witness first-hand the kind of great, consistent, and disciplined marketing that makes a company soar. But as I started to spend more and more time in New York, Naked gained some amazing strategic partners, including three-time NBA champion and fashion icon, Dwyane Wade.

But before I talk about Naked and Team Wade in a second, let me just take a moment and describe what it was like for this small-town kid to move to New York. I'd already been there a dozen times on business trips, but visiting NYC is nothing like living in it. Calling myself a "New Yorker" would have been an insult to the true inhabitants of the world's most famous city—but walking busy streets, hailing taxis, riding the subways at 7:30 am, and eating late into the night had me fantasizing about one day earning such a title. Never before has the energy of place seeped into my veins like the Big Apple. Here I felt like Naked could shoot as high as the endless glass skyscrapers and I'd be right there—on top of the world.
Although it was a challenge, Janna and I loved living in New York. Or at least, living near it—in reality we chose an apartment we thought we could better afford just over the state line in Connecticut, a tiny place above a health food convenience store that later became a pizza parlor. I'd be in the city from morning to night at our new Naked Headquarters on Madison and 29th, and Janna would come

in some evenings for dinner, and of course we'd play tourist every single weekend.

It was an urban fairy tale already, but it went truly surreal when the management team of Dwyane Wade called me.

Why did they call me? Well, a year or so earlier we'd sent some of our underwear to Dwyane and his lovely wife, Gabrielle Union. Both pairs were, in fact, for Dwyane, in the hopes that one of them would actually reach him. They did ... it just took a while!

Apparently he loved them and, having firmly planted himself in the fashion industry, he wanted to meet to discuss collaborating on a Wade X Naked collection of underwear.

His team said that if we could make it down to Miami that week there were courtside seats with our names on them.

I nearly fell out of my chair.

You bet the Naked team was on a plane to Miami and before I knew it I was sitting courtside for the first time in my life, followed by dinner with Dwyane Wade chatting about business and life, in a fancy restaurant open that late only because Dwyane Wade was there.

Before I was ever a runner, basketball was my first love. In Grade 7 I drew a picture of what I wanted to be when I was old and, yup, it was an NBA star. If I ever have the privilege of meeting you, dear reader, and we play a game of 21, you'll see why that dream died shortly thereafter. Now I'm sitting in front of "Flash", my hero, a guy I'd cheered on through three separate championships.

Dwyane to me: "So do you play any ball?"

Me to Dwyane: "Yep."

Dwyane to me: "So how do you shoot?"

Me to Dwyane: "Oh, I hit about nine out of ten shots …"

WAIT. I don't hit nine out of ten shots. Dwyane doesn't hit nine out of ten shots. Nobody hits nine out of ten shots.

Reeling, I add: "Some of the time. The rest of the time I hit one out of ten shots."

With bated breath, I watch Dwyane as he eyes me up and down and then, to my relief, smiles.

Dwyane to me: "You and everyone in the NBA!"

From that moment on I knew that no matter what, we'd be lucky to have someone like Dwyane as a partner. And with Naked now in a financial position to consider this partnership I was determined to do everything I could to make it happen.

Of course, that's not the point of the story. The point of the story is what I learned through our partnership with Dwyane and his team.

As Dwyane worked with many brand partners like Naked, his team took incredible care to ensure not only that the brands he endorsed were both a fit with his personal brand, and also with each other. There were yearly summits and regular calls where Dwyane Wade brand partners all had to take part. They'd walk us through what the Miami Heat were doing and how that tied into their plans. Other brands would share their strategies to ensure things were part of the bigger, overall strategy. Even though we were competing entities with our own corporate cultures and agendas, everyone knew that if a brand partner didn't speak the common language of Brand Wade, what they were building would be in jeopardy. Further, Team Wade didn't just jump on every little opportunity each brand partner offered … even with all the money in the world they were disciplined, consistent and selective. It was incredible to see and be a part of!

Be disciplined with where you spend your marketing dollars. Be disciplined with your messaging and who you're targeting. Just like research-based design, have research-based marketing. Test your marketing ideas before diving deep. In our digital world this is easier and cheaper than ever before.

Everyone is going to have ideas about marketing because almost everyone loves marketing. It's fun to think up ideas and all too easy to convince yourself that your favorite ideas are good ones. But as the boss, you're going to have make hard decisions about where and how to spend those dollars that some people won't like. You're going to have to "not choose" people's ideas sometimes.

The marketing and product development decisions you make early on in a start-up can make or break your company, and to be an effective start-up CEO, you will need to do things that people may not like in the short term.

If you've found product market fit and are consistent and disciplined with your marketing you can, over time, build a great and profitable company. Jim Collins refers to this as building your flywheel. "The process resembles relentlessly pushing a giant, heavy flywheel, turn upon turn, building momentum until a point of breakthrough, and beyond."

7

Finding Balance

Being an entrepreneur isn't just about the business you're building. It's also about how you live your life. Yes, life. That *thing* you intend to have once the business is successful. With that said, this is the point where this little book about entrepreneurship takes a bit of a turn.

Imagine for a moment that you've been in the non-stop hustle of your start-up for a while. You've made the great personal sacrifices required to build your business. Things are moving along but you're not "out of the woods" yet in terms of having a business that can sustain growth on its own revenues. After all, you're still a start-up!

This is the point where you need to check in with yourself, to ensure that your own well-being is looked after.

This is critically important, because if we absorb ourselves completely into our business for too long without caring for our well-being, two problems can arise:

1. We become unhealthy, unhappy and less effective as a business operator;

2. We lose sight of what's truly important in life.

Although it can often feel like it, life isn't all about the business you're building. Among the risks you need to take, the hours you need to put in and the mental attention you need to give the business, there's a whole bunch more of *life* out there that isn't waiting on the sidelines for you to complete your goal or meet your deadline … it's happening right in front of your eyes.

That life includes your family and friends. It includes big celebrations and those little everyday events. Your life outside the business is part of the foundation of your well-being. Balancing these elements can lead to a happier and more prosperous life. Imbalance can seem unimportant at first, or just something to manage, but if left unchecked it will grow until you're hit with burnout, depression, or collapse.

I really can't stress this enough: figuring out your work-life balance as an entrepreneur is essential, both for you and for your business.

My wife Janna is an amazing person, but our relationship hasn't always been (and will never be) perfect—especially when I was burying myself in Naked. There were times, in the early years of both our relationship and the company, when I'd go weeks without feeling like I'd really talked to her, or that every interaction was some disagreement or strained emptiness as my mind and attention were elsewhere.

It was crazy-stressful at work, but I was trying to find some work-life balance by cheering on my local hockey team, the Vancouver Canucks, as they made their most exciting playoff run in years. I managed to get out of the office by six, home in time to watch the game. Janna was quiet as she sat beside me on the couch, a distant look in her eyes with what I assumed was anger about something. I didn't want to face another disagreement about how much I worked, so I lost myself in the hockey game on TV.

The roar from the Canucks crowd was so loud it made the TV shake. Or maybe it was my own feet jumping up and down as I cheered at the top of my lungs, arms raised in victory. What a game! Tying it up in the last twenty seconds to force overtime, and then thirty minutes of nail-biting, sudden death action. And then a fluke rebound handed Kevin Bieksa the puck and he fired it home. The Canucks were going to the Stanley Cup!

I reached over and hugged Janna tight, smothering her face with kisses. Life was amazing! Oh, what sweet release was hockey victory!

I pulled back from her, still grinning.

The distant look in her eyes was still there, and she stared at me with such intensity I felt all the glow of the game snuffed out in an instant. A cold pit formed in my stomach. I sat back, suddenly realizing how uncommunicative she'd been all evening. We'd been up and down for weeks and I should have seen this coming. She was the practical one who put her heart into an education that promised a solid career. No doubt she was finally fed up with my dreaming ways.

I struggled to find my voice. "Janna, what it is?"

The distant look, I suddenly saw, wasn't anger, but fear.

"I'm pregnant."

Then I realized her fear wasn't because she was pregnant but because of my expected reaction. And I regret, with a shame I carried for years, that didn't prove her assumption wrong. I was immediately terrified. I was young, stressed, with a business I desperately wanted to be successful and my only thoughts were how a child might affect those things.

So, yeah … Sometimes life throws a surprise your way. And if your life is out of balance, it can knock you flying.

Hard Work as a Lifestyle

When starting and growing a business, we often tell ourselves an easy lie: it's just another few months like this and then we'll get back to the gym, re-connect with family and friends, and find time to do things that nourish our mind, bodies, and souls. Believing that it will be better then is the lie we often don't know we're telling ourselves. Or as the Indian aphorism states, "What is beyond here, is that which is also here."

We strive to do more, in order to achieve more, in order to get more.

And I'm not going to deny any of this. I've just spent five chapters professing the hard work and sacrifices entrepreneurs need to make to achieve their dreams. This mindset has led to prosperity and abundance for many; millionaires seem to emerge almost overnight and the middle class grows by the hundreds of millions in developing nations.

America is no longer the only land of opportunity and its Dream still beats strong in all us entrepreneurs. If we work hard, promises the Dream, we can have anything we want and do anything we want.

But in the immortal words of productivity guru and author of *Getting Things Done*, David Allen, "You can do anything. But not everything."

This is wisdom for our age, because our culture has for decades been telling us that in order to be *better people* we need to work harder, longer and faster.

When Janna and I first moved to New York, we saw just how true this idea is for the people of that great city. Everybody moves fast and talks fast. I loved the walk from Grand Central Station to the Naked offices because it was the best exercise I got all day. If you want to keep up with New Yorkers, you have to move. I'd stretch out my stride and tear up those sidewalks, feeling the blood pumping in my veins as I went somewhere fast. I'd often be talking on my phone while I walked, feeling important as I accomplished stuff even before I got to my office.

I learned quickly to dodge cars as I dashed across intersections, and to not shout at the drivers if they had the right of way. New Yorkers will push every boundary, but they only really get upset if someone actually breaks the rules.

Once I was approaching an intersection where I actually had a walk signal, so without slowing I stepped out into the street. And nearly got slammed by a cabbie trying to sneak through his red light. Another pedestrian next to me narrowly avoided getting hit, and then stepped right in front of the cab and shouted:

"Whot the fock are you doin'?" (I think that's the postmodern version of "I'm walkin' here!")

Me? I was already moving again, picking up the pace with my phone in hand.

I'd be checking our share price first thing, before reviewing any new daily marketing emails we were sending out and then checking in with my East Coast store buyers. Meetings would pile upon meetings, interrupted only by phone calls, texts, and a few quick emails. And then I could finally connect with Alex and the Abbotsford office way back on the West Coast. By the time they started work it was almost lunch time for me, and I'd still be gaining speed. More meetings, more product reviews, more calls and emails. I'd finally tear myself away from the office around 7:00 (or sometimes 8:00 or even 9:00) and enjoy my power walk back to Grand Central to crowd aboard a commuter train headed for Connecticut. The walk from the local station back up to our apartment was uphill the whole way—one last chance to feel the faintest memory of my running days and burn those quads while squeezing in a few more messages. And then home.

I'd be lucky if Janna was still awake, some nights. And maybe there'd be some dinner wrapped in the fridge for me. Our baby, Quinn, was getting better at sleeping during the night, but Janna was just always so tired. Some weeks I'm sure it felt like she was a single mom—those same weeks I spent so much time in the city that I might as well have been on the other side of the country. We weren't doing many weekend tourist visits anymore (just getting Quinn packed up to take to the park at the end of our road was exhausting) and date nights were nothing but a distant memory.

I knew that Janna was trying her best, and if she was still up she'd always smile, give me a kiss and try to have a normal conversation. I would usually try back, but my mind was always so full of work stuff that I struggled to think of anything else to talk about. Naked was the center of my universe, just like Quinn was the center of Janna's. I was dimly aware of what was happening, but how could I possibly slow down *now*? Naked was so close to success!

There was a time when work was simply a civic duty or a means to provide for your family. Then we went from a culture of "working to live" to one where, instead, we "lived to work". Success was an equation of effort. *Hard work* became a brand, a badge of honor, a measure of good character.

Hard work practically became a maxim. Although it has much value, truth, and necessity, we accepted it without context. We didn't modify it as the times we lived in changed, and the ways we conducted our *hard work* evolved.

The internet, globalized competition, and our digital devices now encourage 24/7 connectivity as the rule not the exception. According to a Deloitte Research Study, in 2016 Americans checked their phones fifty times a day. New research suggests that it's now eighty times a day … or every 12 minutes.

Working through lunch and breaks, on evenings and weekends is something the vast majority of Americans now do. Another study in 2014 showed that in America an average of 5.7 vacation days were unused by the end of the year and a Gallup report showed 18 percent of Americans consistently work over 60 hours a week.

We adopted the belief that we should be invincible. Rest or sleep was for the weak. Vacations were for the lazy. Endless ambition was a greater virtue than genuine contentment.

And to the frantic entrepreneur, doesn't this make sense? We have so much to do! There are deadlines to meet, meetings to attend, emails to answer, podcasts to listen to, posts to make, social threads to engage in! Our endless to-do lists are always there, waiting for us to cross a few items off them.

The Need for Balance

What our society didn't realize, though, was that for many of us this volume of work was counterproductive. It leads not to success but to burnout, and burnout leads to unproductiveness, procrastination, lack of patience, feeling overwhelmed, frequent sickness and lack of motivation.

There was a study done way back in 1940, which measured men working at the Bethlehem Steel Company who loaded pig iron onto freight train cars. The study set up the men in two scenarios.

Scenario One had the men working non-stop until they loaded 12.5 tons. By midday, they were so exhausted they couldn't load any more. In Scenario Two the men loaded for 26 minutes and then rested for 34 minutes. By resting more than working they ended up loading 47 tons (four times as much!) by the end of day.

Great, you might say, but this seems so counter-intuitive to what we're taught about hard work. Too many entrepreneurs ignore the lesson of Bethlehem Steel, don't maintain a work-life balance, and ultimately get the exact opposite result of what they intended.

Data from The American Institute of Stress in New York estimates that job stress costs the United States economy some $300 billion in sick-time, long-term disability, and excessive job turnover.

So I hope you're getting my point here: constant, frantic work won't make you or your company more productive, and it will actually lead in time to negative results.

But you're an entrepreneur with a dream! You have passion, energy and vision! How can you possibly slow down, or make time for non-business activities?

I'm reminded of my days toiling as a long-distance runner. Always determined to out-train my competitors, I'd run extra miles after practice (sometimes sneaking these in after everyone had left) or doing another mini-workout when I got home. I'd constantly visualize races at night and obsess over my training logs, never giving my mind a break. I'd refuse to take breaks in the off-season to properly recover. School parties and other fun events I viewed as a waste of energy, so I attended none.

I couldn't stop myself. In my obsession to be the fastest, I couldn't accept what my coaches constantly preached about the difference between working hard and working smart.

Ultimately this was my undoing, as I eventually tore my Achilles. Not only was my body so burned out that healing took much longer than it should have, but I realized that I'd lost the will to even carry on running. Because of my years of obsessively driving myself, I'd lost all joy in a sport that I'd once loved dearly. My 117-lb body was so completely wrecked that even the possibility of returning to the sport was out of the question. I'd pushed myself so hard, mentally and physically, that my mind and body had nothing left.

Yet the answers to my well-being, and maybe even greater success in my sport, had been right in front of me the whole time. The answer was more rest and better balance in my life. I just figured it out too late.

Balance, in any endeavor, is found through the trifecta of our Body, Spirit, and Mind.

Body – We maintain a healthy body by exercising regularly, eating reasonably healthy and getting enough sleep.

Spirit – We maintain a healthy spirit by having meaningful relationships with the people we love. Doing what we love nourishes our spirit. We can achieve a healthier spirit by staying true to our personal beliefs, having a sense of connection to higher powers and being in nature.

Mind – We maintain a healthy mind by both continuing to learn new things and taking a break from work thoughts. This can come from meditation, reading, hobbies, and taking time to unplug and be silent.

Ultimately, what gives you balance will be personal to you—we're all different and we each have to uncover our unique passions. Sometimes one activity, such as rock climbing or playing a competitive sport, might hit all three elements of the trifecta as it can be physical and mentally challenging, and also keep you connected to a community. If time is a scarce commodity, which it usually is for the entrepreneur, it's a great idea to find activities that blend these elements together.

You can find ways to bring these elements into your work environment, too. You can work out with your colleague and discuss business at the same time or have "walking" meetings out in nature. My friend, a business coach named Cameron Brown out of Australia, calls this blending. Naturally, whenever he and I meet to discuss ideas and catch up, we go for super long walks.

Blending is a brilliant way to maximize your time, just so long as you're feeling the benefits of balance in the activities you're doing. If combining the "work" piece takes away too much from the activity, you won't experience as much of the balancing effect.

When our Body, Spirit, and Mind are balanced, we're better positioned to thrive and feel happy—when they're unbalanced, we suffer.

Being motivated and driven to work hard is actually the easy part. There are always more emails, contracts and sales calls, and we're conditioned to just have another coffee and push through the fatigue. We're terrified to stop, just for a day, a week or even a month because we're afraid that if we do, the whole house of cards will come crashing down on us.

(It usually won't, by the way—it'll just be waiting there tomorrow, just as urgent as it was today or yesterday.)

The reality is that constant stress and overwork is ultimately unsustainable, even for the youngest and healthiest of entrepreneurs. Lack of sleep is an epidemic with consequences that range from memory to mood to performance and beyond. Chronic overwork and stress expose our bodies to unhealthy levels of adrenaline and cortisol. Plenty of studies have shown that these can increase your risk of heart disease and cardiovascular disease. Not mention colds, flus, depression and anxiety. [3]

Consider this Chinese proverb: "If you listen to your body when it whispers, you won't have to hear it scream."

In my early years of running Naked, I unfortunately didn't do this. In the early years, when things seemed impossible, I'd just remind myself of a conversation between Batman and Alfred:

Batman: "What would you have me do, Alfred?"

Alfred: "Endure, Master Wayne."

It seemed so noble, so selfless, so heroic. Sacrificing myself for the good of the company. I was young, I was strong, I was determined. I could do anything. That philosophy worked … until it didn't.

I don't remember exactly which crisis I was grappling with at the time. It might have been a problem with the color of an entire batch of product which we'd already shipped, or it might have been

 3 British Heart Foundation. (n.d.) Feeling Stressed? Research Shows How Stress Can Lead to Heart Attacks and Stroke. Heart Matters. Retrieved from: https://www.bhf.org.uk/informationsupport/heart-matters-magazine/news/behind-the-headlines/stress-and-heart-disease

another terrible deal being offered to me by loan shark "investors". Or, probably, it was some combination of both. I don't remember exactly what was weighing down my thoughts—I just remember the sharp agonizing pain that erupted in my head as I collapsed in a heap in the shower.

Janna was home, thankfully, and I must have cried out because the next thing I knew the water stopped pouring down on me and I was looking up dimly into her eyes. Those liquid orbs of beautiful, greenish grey were laced with fear, but her voice was calm as she helped me up, toweled me off, got me dressed and down to the car. She was trained as a nurse and doula so this was nothing she hadn't seen before.

The emergency ward at the hospital was a blur, but I remember being surprised at how quickly I was processed and in a bed with IV's hooked up to me. That should have been my first clue of how serious things were.

I was stripped down and put in a hospital gown, although I was able to keep my Naked boxer briefs on (the pathetic part of me couldn't help but wonder if the nurses noticed "those awesome boxers that dude is wearing"). I was stabilized quickly—the IV was morphine, I learned—and I was able to take stock of the situation before I started to slide into a dreamy state.

Janna was still at my side, Quinn in her arms. She had my cell phone and I eventually asked why it kept chiming.

"It's Alex," she said, "wanting to know if you're okay."

"I'm fine. Ask him if he's had a chance to review that term sheet from the new investor group."

I'd been stressing about that issue as Alex and I were in unusual territory, embroiled in a month-long disagreement about two specific investor opportunities and which one was right for Naked.

Janna didn't answer, and even through my drug-induced fog I could sense the sudden change in the air. I glanced at her. She was staring at me, tears in her eyes.

"What?" I asked.

"You collapsed … And now you're hospitalized with meningitis. And your first thought is about some stupid term sheet?"

I was beyond feeling pain at that point, but my wife's words cut right to my heart. Normally I'd either dismiss them or defend myself, talk about how whatever business task I was doing was so important. But as I lay there on that bed, morphine trickling into my wrist, blue curtains around us and the hubbub of a medical center just beyond, I suddenly saw the world with new clarity.

Janna was right. Raising money didn't matter right now. Fixing inventory didn't matter right now. Hell, the entire company didn't matter right now. She could see that; Alex could see that—apparently I was the only one who was blind.

Laying there in that bed, I asked myself the question: why was I doing this to myself?

Obviously collapsing due to exhaustion and stress wasn't helping me, my family, or my shareholders. And it wasn't like this was the first time I'd been to the hospital since starting Naked. And each time it was getting worse. Exhaustion and hypertension I could recover from. So I now had meningitis? I'm sure, if I took care of myself, I could recover from that. But what would be next? I wouldn't be able to undo a heart attack, or walk off a stroke.

I could continue to push, to sacrifice myself for my company. But what for? As I stared at Janna, wiping her eyes as she angrily put my phone away, it was finally clear to me that I needed to make fundamental changes, and I needed to make them now.

Listen, dear reader, and take a good look at yourself. I don't want you to get to this place. Ever.

Finding Balance

There will be periods of time where you're deep in a "work bender" (as Alex and I called them) with no time to surface for air. There are deadlines to meet and opportunities to seize! Working your butt off to meet a deadline, producing a beautiful product, and breaking into a new market are incredibly rewarding experiences. Having a sense of purpose or passion in your business makes even a few years in the hard work trenches feel energizing and can make the "earned" rest, as I once heard it said, you do take that much sweeter. That said, at some point the tank will run out unless you've maintained balance in your life. To do this you'll need to build in periods where you have lower stress, more rest, and more down time to take care of yourself.

During my most intense year training as a runner we called this periodization, where periods of rest were built into our training programs to allows our muscles and bodies to recover and grow stronger. Without these rest periods most athletes I knew would either plateau in their development or burnout entirely.

There's an obvious (if self-defeating) response to this idea: I don't have the time or flexibility to achieve work-life balance.

This might seem to be true, but it's all a matter of perspective and choice. Remember, you're an entrepreneur and you control your own schedule. You control what people can and can't expect of your time. If you answer every email as soon as it blasts into your inbox, you're establishing the expectation of your response time. If you tell your team or customers that you only respond to emails during three 1-hour periods during the day (or even every second day) then that's what they'll expect and they won't be chasing you unless something's really urgent.

You need to change the conversation you're having with yourself about your time, what you really need to do and why that matters—to you and to your business.

Vilfredo Pareto was an Italian economist who gave us Pareto's Law. You'll know this law as the 80/20 Rule. The law states that essentially 80% of your business comes from 20% of your customers or products. I reference that here because the same law applies to your time. You'll find that much of your work time is consumed by too many emails, meetings you don't need to be in, dealing with HR issues or admin tasks. In other words, you're probably spending most (80%) of your time on stuff that doesn't produce results. Herein lies the individual task of assessing what aspects of your time spent on work are necessary and yield high results versus what's just busy work that can be stopped (or assigned to someone else) so that you have more time for balance.

If you think you have no time for balance because you NEED TO ALWAYS WORK HARDER EVERY MINUTE OF THE DAY, just remember that this kind of work ethic is built on a lie. Working hard isn't the same as working smart, rest is not weakness, and over the long term a balanced existence is essential for survival.

Remember, too, that you don't have to do everything NOW. Once, when I explained to a colleague my feelings of angst about trying to prioritize everything, he shared with me a passage from Ecclesiastes 3 that I found solace in.

There is an appointed time for everything,

and a time for every affair under the heavens.

A time to give birth, and a time to die;

a time to plant, and a time to uproot the plant.

A time to kill, and a time to heal;

a time to tear down, and a time to build.

A time to weep, and a time to laugh;

a time to mourn, and a time to dance.

A time to scatter stones, and a time to gather them;

a time to embrace, and a time to be far from embraces.

A time to seek, and a time to lose;

a time to keep, and a time to cast away.

A time to rend, and a time to sew;

a time to be silent, and a time to speak.

A time to love, and a time to hate;

a time of war, and a time of peace.

What profit have workers from their toil?

I have seen the business that God has given to mortals to be busied about.

God has made everything appropriate to its time, but has put the timeless into their hearts so they cannot find out, from beginning to end, the work which God has done.

I recognized that there is nothing better than to rejoice and to do well during life.

Moreover, that all can eat and drink and enjoy the good of all their toil—this is a gift of God.

There's a time for everything, and some things can wait.

You have the same amount of time as anyone else, but as an entrepreneur you have a lot more freedom, or should I say flexibility, to decide how you spend it.

People are Worth More than Companies

Consider also your relationships. Whether it's your children, spouse, boyfriend/girlfriend, or friends, your relationships take time, effort, and attention to be successful and fulfilling. A good relationship can lift our spirits, fill us with love and give us a sense of community and place. But these very precious human connections are what we often take the most for granted.

To put it bluntly, just because you're married doesn't mean you'll stay married if you don't take the time to stay deeply connected with your spouse.

Those we choose to have relationships with should in turn support us in our endeavors. If your partner tells you to quit pursuing your passion and go get a "real" job (a.k.a. a job with normal working hours like the customary 9-5) then they obviously don't know you and they may not be the right partner. Listen to their concerns, of course, and make sure you're clear about your own priorities. Remember, we're talking balance—the give and take in our relationships. Find ways to support each other and change as individuals. You need to support your partners, friends, and spouses through this, and in turn they'll support you.

If you have children, your money, success, and accomplishments will mean very little to them. It's your presence and attention that matter. Studies have shown that children who feel safe and secure in their relationship with their parent enjoy a massive uplift in their development. It's known to improve linguistic and mental development, as well as emotional development that helps children deal with stress. [4]

Many studies have also shown that the first five years of a child's life

 4 Parenting NI. (2018, October 25). Parent-Child Relationship—Why It's Important. [web log post]. Parenting NI. Retrieved from: https://www.parentingni.org/blog/parent-child-relationship-why-its-important/

are crucial in terms of them establishing this connection. [5] You can't do that from your office desk or with eyes locked on a computer screen.

Creating a sense of home in your family relationships can also have wonderful balancing effects on your life.

Graham Rowles, a gerontology professor at the University of Kentucky says: "There is pretty strong evidence that the environment in which people live is closely linked to their well-being. It's sort of like the human animal attachment to territory is built into our DNA. Home provides security, control, belonging, identity. But most of all, it's a place that provides us with a centering—a place from which we leave each morning and to which we return each evening."

Your work schedule may not mean you can spend eight hours a day with your spouse or children, nor am I suggesting that you should. Your work is important. Your commitment to your passion and purpose is important. It doesn't have to be one or the other, though. When you spend time with those you love you need to be conscious of how present you are with them during the time you do have.

No matter how bad or good a day you had at work, you need to drop it all and be fully there with them. If you're going to make love with your spouse, then make sure they feel all your love and attention. If you're playing with your children—truly make it a time to remember … connecting deeply with them on their level. Don't spend the one time you see your best friend each month on your phone posting social media.

Give your energy to these people in your life. They'll cherish your less-frequent presence more than a whole lot of un-present time where you're just taking calls and checking email.
Lastly, minimize those after-work social functions with your colleagues. Knowing how much time you need to give to your business, its employees, and customers during the day, remember to spend as much of your "fun time" with your family or close friends as possible.

5 Tomlinson, A. (2015). Why the First Five Years of a Child's Development Are the Most Important. The National. Retrieved from: https://www.thenational.ae/arts-culture/why-the-first-five-years-of-a-child-s-development-are-the-most-important-1.127401

I say this all not wanting to discourage someone from starting a business because they have young children or a new relationship. The point I'm making here is to not fall into the trap of sacrificing your relationships in the present for some glorious future. The present is all you have. As my father once shared with me from The Gospel of Luke:

"A rich man had a fertile farm that produced fine crops. He said to himself, 'What should I do? I don't have room for all my crops.' Then he said, 'I know! I'll tear down my barns and build bigger ones. Then I'll have room enough to store all my wheat and other goods. And I'll sit back and say to myself, "My friend, you have enough stored away for years to come. Now take it easy! Eat, drink, and be merry!"'

"But God said to him, 'You fool! You will die this very night. Then who will get everything you worked for?'

"Yes, a person is a fool to store up earthly wealth but not have a rich relationship with God."

Luke: 12:16-21

This brings me to the final point of this chapter on balance—focus on what's truly important in life.

Remember how I said the book was going to take a turn here? Well if you don't think it has already, what I'm going to say next may make your entrepreneurial insides twist with discomfort. And it may seem contradictory to everything I've said about starting a business and following your purpose and passion.

Here it is.

Your business is important, but it's not the most important thing in your life. In fact, it's a fleeting thing to attach yourself to.
What I'm asking you to see now is that your family, your physical and mental health, and your relationships are more important than

your company. At the end of the day, when the crowds stop cheering, the press stops talking about you and the deals stop flowing, it's your personal relationships, and not your company, that are what you'll still be with. Your family and children will most likely outlast your business.

To any outside observer, my family was living the dream. We had an apartment on the beautiful and posh Greenwich Ave in Connecticut. I worked on Madison Ave, posted photos of spectacular Manhattan date nights in Instagram, frequently traveled between Vancouver and New York, and enjoyed working vacations in Florida and the Caribbean.

That was the good. And it was freaking cool!

The bad was that I also traveled extensively and had been for years. If I wasn't commuting two and half hours each day to and from the city, getting home around midnight and leaving the next day around 7:00 am, I'd be in Chicago, Miami, LA, or oversees. In fact, I traveled over two hundred days in each of the first two years of my daughter's life.

When I was home with my family, I'd stop mid-playtime to take calls from investors or my colleagues—weekends included.

Morning would see me on my phone at the breakfast table and whenever the kids weren't looking I'd do the same at the parks, on vacation, or just hanging out.

This, understandably, had put my marriage on the verge.

Then three things happened. First, I bumped into an old friend named Nikos. Nikos had invented a "rehabilitation technique" called micro stretching and had helped rehab a few of my running injuries. We hadn't spoken in years and when we reconnected I had coffee with him to catch up.

He told me how a certain person had requested a meeting for our time slot but that he'd told this person he couldn't meet. When I heard who it was, unbeknownst to my friend, that person happened to be a huge celebrity in the fitness and health world. HUGE. I informed Nikos of who that person was and that he should have blown me off to secure that meeting.

Nikos looked at me sternly and said that no one is more important than anyone else, especially your friends and family. He then told me how he always told this to his A-List sports clients who wanted his therapies right away.

I, in contrast, had been guilty of interrupting my own daughter for some banker I barely knew because I thought he could give my company money.

My chance reconnection with Nikos helped me begin to shift my behaviors.

Although this had made things a little better, I continued burning the candle at both ends and ended up in hospital yet again. This was the second event.

Stomach pains and more headaches ensued to the point where I was keeled over with what the doctor thought was kidney stones. It wasn't—my stomach seemed to be the place where my deepest stress and anxiety liked to manifest in agonizing pain. I was given morphine tablets, a cortisol shot for the pressure in my head, and was made to drink a thick, foul-tasting liquid to coat my stomach.

Janna, usually so caring and supportive, didn't visit me during this trip to the hospital. I'd done this to myself—that was the lesson Janna was teaching me and she wasn't prepared to continue accepting this behavior. My body wasn't whispering anymore … it was screaming.

I sat by myself in another hospital bed as the full weight of this realization penetrated my soul. It hurt. But I was starting to realize what I had to do ...

If that wasn't enough, a third thing happened to provide one final lesson to finally make me realize I needed to change. Barely recovered from my stomach issues and about to leave for Texas on a business trip, I got the phone call I wouldn't have expected in a million years.

Cam, my beach body counting friend, the guy who'd complimented me on building a great team, and who had personally invested in Naked when the company had needed it most, had passed away.

Cam hadn't been sick. He wasn't old. He was young and had a wife and two beautiful baby girls.

It was too much to take, but at this point all I knew about how to react was to be like Bruce Wayne and endure. The next morning, devastated and my heart impossibly heavy, I headed to San Antonio for business meetings.

All day long I put on the face I needed to for each meeting ... giving everyone the tiny crumbs of what energy I had left in me. When I got back to the hotel, I poured myself a whiskey and sat on the patio. The humid air kissing my skin, I sat staring out across the hotel parking lot at a city I didn't know or want to be in.

Finally allowed to cry, the tears began to pour down my face. Flooded with thoughts of Cam, his family, his girls, his business partner, the precious gift of this one awesome life we have and those we get to spend it with. I finally, finally knew that I had to change my priorities in life.

As I sat there on that San Antonio hotel balcony, sipping at a whiskey as tears dried on my cheeks, I recalled something I'd heard on the radio just a week before. I often had noise in the background as I worked, but this story had stopped me in my tracks. I'd listened, spellbound, and on that Texas balcony I thought back over it.

The story was told by a woman about speaking to her husband on the phone during the last 30 minutes of his life—he was trapped in the World Trade Center when it collapsed on September 11th.

They certainly didn't talk about his work. They didn't talk about his successes and recognitions. They talked about love and the moments of their lives together.

He was choking on smoke and by the end of the conversation he could only whisper and tell his wife he loved her—over and over again.

When she heard a loud crash, "like an avalanche," she knew the building had collapsed. Her husband was gone.

She didn't hang up the phone. And despite it being the most tragic day of her life she didn't want the day to end … because it was still a day that her husband had been alive. For it was only hours before that he had kissed her and gone to work.

As soon as she went to bed that day would be over.

When I recalled this story, I started crying again. Had Cam and his wife had those final moments to talk about love? Would I have those final moments with Janna? She'd already made it clear that she wasn't coming to the hospital for me again. So how much longer was I going to push? And what was I pushing for? A business?

In the hot Texas air I finally saw things for what they were. How I was working myself toward an early grave, how I was sacrificing the present for an unknown future. I could feel the work tension wrapped up tight inside me, could feel the pressures of business weighing me down. But none of that mattered if I didn't have what was most important to me.

I took a deep breath in, held it for a moment, then exhaled. And again. I closed my eyes and kept breathing, and with each breath I focused on my wife and children, and exhaled out all the unnecessary stress that I'd been taking on for years. I realized just how tightly I'd been holding onto the wrong things, and I started to let them go. With each exhale, I started to let go.

The next night, when I returned home to New York, I hugged my wife and children and cried again. If it had been me in that tower, I knew I wouldn't have cared how much money was in my bank account or how our new product was being received in stores. Memories of my children's lives would be what I thought of first; moments with my wife, adventures with some of my dearest friends, and time with my own parents and family. That, I'm sure, is what they'd remember too.

And I told Janna that night that I was going to change.

I asked myself, why I was working this much? I thought of Ernest Becker's Pulitzer-Prize-winning book *The Denial of Death*, which explains how the meaning of our lives is too often shaped by our desire to leave something behind, to prove that we existed and, by doing so, to never truly die. Becker calls these "Immortality Projects."

I realized that I was guilty of wanting a legacy. We celebrate the hell out of legacies, but are they really that all-important? What if we don't get the plaque on the wall, the record in the record books, or star on that TV special?

As Becker says, "The greatness in our lives comes not from our 'immortality project' but from caring for something greater than ourselves." Immortality projects suck all intention inward ... they breed entitlement. They create the need to feel GREAT.

Living and working in New York had been amazing. Closing deals. Being recognized for contributions. Making money and having people praise me about all the success. It gave me a sense of identity.

But this identity and these accomplishments were fleeting. Not just because businesses fail, or because legacies may not really mean that much in the grand scheme of things. No, it was because they were taking away the life I was living now.

Work is a good thing. In fact, it's a great thing. But it's not the only thing and it's certainly not the most important thing in your life. My priorities shifted immediately toward work-life balance and re-connection with my family.

The first change: When I was home with my family, I would be just that, home. We became more regimented with the use of our phones (especially in front of our kids), and I even took eight months away from social media.

Personally, this allowed for healthier routines such as daily journaling, exercise, and meditation. Although it took time, these habits eventually helped my head to clear, my immunity to improve and for me to re-connect with my passion for entrepreneurship and life.

I tried to not get caught up in the busy details of the everyday grind and eventually I could take full days to focus completely on singular tasks—no phones, messages, calls, just incredibly productive, creative work.

All in all, the changes in balance took over three years and admittedly are still a work in progress. But it was step in the right direction.

Although it can be one of the hardest things to do, balance is the secret in your success formula. Like all good investments and strategies, the payoff may take time to notice but it will be happening—even before you know it.

We must keep the health of our body, mind, and spirit at the forefront of all we do. Rest and work. Rest and grow. Rest and thrive. This is how you're designed. Building the principle of balance into your work schedule, your team's scheduling, and your overall business development will lead to more fulfilling and successful lives—

success not just defined by profit and productivity but also by the quality of your relationships, your happiness, and your life.

8

Dealing with Radical Change

As your business grows from an idea to an actual start-up with real money behind it, revenues and products or services, and the buzzing daily activity of something resembling a profitably growing company—or alternatively to something that didn't really work the way you wanted it to—you're going to experience change. Sometimes radical change.

Up until now we've looked at a lot of the "nuts and bolts" issues that you'll deal with as an entrepreneur—how to get started, how to raise money, how to hire well, how to build processes, and even the importance of balance in your work. These things will all bring change to your business, but they're part of the creation process and are intended to bring stability.

But let's be honest with ourselves, life isn't stable or predictable at all, is it? The radical change I'm talking about in this chapter comes later in the process, after you've already built your business into something relatively solid. Radical change can sometimes be driven by growth, and sometimes by chance, but sooner or later, it will strike.

Each entrepreneurial journey is unique, and I can't predict everything that will happen on yours, but in this chapter I'd like to talk about some of the big changes that you can expect and how to prepare for them.

Adversity is Inevitable

Generally, I'm a believer in being optimistic when approaching business and life. That said, we also need to be realists and recognize that life has a way of sending us our fair dose of adversity. Even if you hire well, if you have great values, principles and objectives, if your "Why" is clear and your processes are solid, you will still sometimes fail.

These failures could be a result of how you did things at your company, your strategy, or even the vision of the company itself. They could also be because you couldn't get proper financing, had a fight with your partner or board, or the local economic conditions change.

Hopefully, the failures are just little tasks or missteps. Maybe you lose an important account, deliver a product that has defects, or miss a launch date. Big or small, detrimental to your business or a blip on the radar, whatever the failure is, you need to go into business understanding and accepting that it will happen.

Even success brings change, though, and it can be as stressful as a failure. Your little one-person show working out of your dining room will bear little resemblance to a team of professionals working in an office. Plain and simple—with scale comes issues: what matters is how you deal with and grow from adversity.

First of all, take ownership of your mistakes. Hire people that take ownership of theirs. Taking ownership of mistakes isn't always easy. Even a little failure in a start-up feels huge.

Second, maintain perspective. The stakes are high, but remember that they're never as high as they seem. The first failure is always terrible. You think there's great giant light shining on your failure … but really, no one cares … really. Like really, really. And if they do care it's probably only for a few seconds before the next shiny object grabs their attention. But it's so easy to internalize and become self-absorbed in our failure—I was guilty of thinking everyone in the known world would think me an idiot for things I failed at in my business.

Stop. Separate yourself from the failure. Just a little separation. Often when I'm absorbed in the self-destructive thoughts of my own failure, I try to take the perspective of a person looking at me, and I try to offer genuine advice as that outsider to my troubled self. Just like we're able to bring rational judgment and compassion when our friends seek our counsel and comfort for their own problems, we do have the same capacity with ourselves. Your objective as a human being and business operator is to do the best you can until you know how to do it better. Then once you know a little better you do better, again, again, and again.

Every small failure along the way is only one thing and nothing more—you have an entire business to run and a life to live. Failure also teaches resilience. You're the sum of your parts but you're not defined by the mistakes of the past, as you're the one who creates your story moving forward. So keep perspective and remember the grand vision you're building toward. A failure doesn't block your path, it only becomes a part of it. It's just a step along the way that helps shape you and your company to be a better operator, manager, and decision-maker in the future.

At Naked, when we failed at something and were feeling low about it, Alex and I always used to do a "check in" with each other. We'd go for a walk to try and shift any stagnant energy from our funk and agree that: "We're glad to be here." We'd then list things we were grateful for about the business and finally debrief what went wrong and how to improve it for next time.

Encourage and support your team members in finding their own ways to "shake off" their failures and move forward.

I like to take what I think is a Zen Buddhist approach to failure. Something is neither a failure nor a success—it's only how we view things. We're taught to fear failure. We're taught this because our society only celebrates success. Why don't we celebrate failures?

Some companies in the Silicon Valley and Silicon Alley have already adopted this mindset and they've even been known to have Failure Parties!

"Cheers to that royal fuck up! … Now, what did you learn?"

When something doesn't go as planned, the only question is: "What are you going to do about it?"

To paraphrase the philosopher Alain de Botton, "If you're not embarrassed by who you were 12 months ago—you didn't learn enough."

Losing Key Partners

I certainly didn't build Naked all by myself. Some people were partners on my journey for a short time, or for a specific purpose. But others were in it for the long haul—trusted friends and teammates who shared my passion and vision, and who were invaluable to me.

You'll probably have key partners in your entrepreneurial journey, too. You come to rely on them, and probably think that they'll always be there. It can be quite a shock when you suddenly discover that they're leaving. I remember like it was yesterday when I received a fateful call. I was travelling, as usual, and I happened to be in my Florida hotel room when the phone buzzed.

"Hello?"

"Hey, Joel—it's Alex."

Something was up. I could tell in just those four words. For one, after all these years he really didn't need to introduce himself.

"Hey, man. What's going on?"

"Do you have a few minutes?"

"Yeah, I'm done my store visits for the day. What's up?"

There was a pause on the line, then: "Joel, I'm sorry. I have to resign my position at Naked."

The words were received in my brain, but I really, truly didn't understand what they meant for a very long moment.

"Hello?" Alex said.

"Yeah, I'm here."

Another pause.

"Joel, this isn't how I wanted things to go, but ultimately I have to think of my career. Naked is going to be fine—I believe it will happen for you. But right now I don't agree with the choices you're making with those new investors and I have a lot to lose if this goes bankrupt because of a choice I didn't agree with. So I've decided to take another job."

I slid the phone away from my mouth and exhaled deeply. I didn't have the energy to fight. I didn't want to fight.

"But Alex, I need you on the team."

"I don't know if you do, Joel. Three times in the last six months you've gone against my strongest recommendations on how to get capital funding, and three times I think your decision has put the company in greater risk. I'm not sure what use I still am to you."

Alex wasn't angry, I could tell. If anything, there was a resigned sadness in his voice.

"When are you going to leave?" I asked. "Are you quitting right now?"

"No, no, of course not. I can stay two more weeks and make sure Julie and Sandra are up to speed on everything."

"I have to finish this trip."

"I know. Do you want me to tell the team now, or when you get back?"

I couldn't believe I was actually having this conversation. It was like a dream, so calm, so quiet, and so completely out of my control. I didn't think for a second that I'd be able to change Alex's mind. Alex didn't make decisions like this without having thought through every angle.

"We'll tell them when I'm back," I said.

"Yeah," Alex said softly. "I'm going to hate that moment."

I heard another silence stretch out. It was hard to even think of anything to say.

"Do you want to talk later?" Alex asked.

"I don't know," I said. "Probably. But not right now."

"Okay, man. Call me any time."

The call ended. I dropped the phone away from my ear, staring up at the cracked ceiling of the cheap motel room.

I'd lost people before. Travis had decided to go another way. My two biggest early investors had turned away when it became too much trouble. My first board chair had left when the liabilities became too much.

But Alex. Alex had been there pretty much right from the beginning. He'd endured years of poor pay, long hours, and taken more than his share of stakeholder wrath to protect me.
Even now, he was the pillar of the Naked team, the manager who was the real leader of the awesome team in Abbotsford.

How the fuck was Naked going to survive without Alex?

Without giving myself a moment to think, I changed into my running gear, grabbed my keys, and headed out the door.

The afternoon sun was glorious, the heat pouring down on my aching muscles as I crossed the busy street and picked up into a jog. It was at least two miles through Tampa to the waterfront, but my legs churned forward. My body reveled in the surge of energy, my mind focusing on nothing but pushing my body harder and faster. No time for thinking. Just run.

I could see and hear the jetliners overhead as I ran, and I knew I was getting close. Finally, the rows of office buildings gave way to a wide green space, and beyond it was a wooden path leading down to the beach. I accelerated over the rough grass, drawing on ancient reserves as a long-distance runner for that last sprint toward the finish line. The grass disappeared as my feet thundered onto the wooden planks, then sand was kicking up around me and the waters of the Gulf of Mexico stretched out to the horizon.

I slowed to a jog, then finally to a walk, sucking in great gulps of warm, moist air. The sea breeze danced over my sweat-soaked skin and the echo of my heartbeat thudded in my ears. I stared out at the sparkling blue water, watched as another aircraft roared down overhead to land.

Another batch of travellers, I thought. Probably a plane-load of sun seekers or unconnected, weary business people like me, making yet another stop in their endless rounds of the stores or clients. I'd always loved the being in motion, and being on the road so much had kept me inspired. This time, though, it just felt like a never-ending march with no point and no ending. I watched the next plane descend, probably sixty seconds after the first, delivering in turn its cargo of human beings. It was a tough life, being an entrepreneur.

I walked along the sand until my heart had slowed and my breathing had mellowed, then I found a broad rock to sit down on. As I stared out along the Tampa shoreline I concentrated on my breathing and stilled my mind.

This was what I'd chosen for myself years ago when I'd set out to be an entrepreneur. There had been no shortage of opportunities to take on a normal life, like Travis had, I mused with a pang of envy, and there had even been opportunities to sell my fledgling dream and walk away. But I never had.

And as I closed my eyes, concentrating on my breathing, I knew why this was so. Yes, I wanted to see if I could do it—build something from nothing but a flash of inspiration and a lucky stop in a damn night market in Peru. Yes, I wanted to make a difference. I'd had a vision of what I wanted to accomplish with Naked, and I'd believed in it so much that no obstacle had been too big to stop me.

Alex had believed in the vision—he'd sacrificed his own promising career as an accountant at a great firm to join Naked—and he'd stood side by side with me through adversities that still give me nightmares. But ultimately, I realized, the vision of Naked wasn't Alex's. It wasn't Janna's, or that of my investors.

It was my vision. And I was going to see it through. No matter what.

Remember this, when or if you lose key partners. Your business is your vision, not anyone else's. No matter how important or essential another person is to your business, you have to remember that they have other priorities in their life, and they may not always prioritize like you do. You'll no doubt have great and loyal partners, like Alex, who stick with the company through all sorts of storms. Those people are precious and you want to do everything you can to keep them motivated and onside … But life may very well have other plans and if they're going to leave you have to be ready for it—mentally, spiritually, and professionally. And if they make the decision, don't stop them—once the heart isn't in it, there's no point trying to convince them to stay. There are other talented, hard working people out there who can fill those shoes.

Have a back-up plan for any of your key partners—try to ensure that they aren't a single point of failure in your company. If they leave, who can take over their role, even temporarily? The answer to that might be "you" but you're already busy enough. As you grow your team, build in some basic overlap of responsibilities as best you can, so that different teammates can cover for each other when necessary.

And be emotionally ready for it. It hurts when a key partner leaves. It's easy to feel betrayed or abandoned, but that's mostly your fear talking. If you've built your team well and have strong lines of communication, you probably won't be surprised when a key partner decides to leave, but sometimes people play their cards close to their chest. Sometimes a key partner will hide their intentions to leave in order to protect you, because they might be feeling guilt and might not want to face the moment any more than you. Each situation will play out differently—all I'm saying is, be ready. Try not to get upset. Try to make your first reaction a "thank you" for all the time and energy they've dedicated to your dream. You'll have to grieve their departure at some point, I'm sure, but in the immediate aftermath you'll need to acknowledge your feelings but rise above them to complete the transition task at hand. Your team will look to you for optimism during these times and if you can't provide it fear will seep in amongst the ranks.

And then, once you've had time to process this new reality, your feelings included, start to rebuild. Losing a partner is radical change, but it doesn't mean the end.

The Founder's Dilemma

Key partners are an important part of a company, but none of them are as important as you, the founder. As founder of the company you'll bring a lot to the table—passion, determination, vision, and sometimes even expertise. But what makes any founder a great CEO in the start-up days may not translate into the founder being the best choice to lead the company as it grows and transitions. There are famous examples, like Bill Gates and Mark Zuckerberg, who were able to grow with their companies and remain at the helm through many stages of growth—but more often than not, this isn't the case.

What will likely happen, at some point or another as your company grows, is that you'll face the Founder's Dilemma: are you still the best person to lead your company?

I'd come under criticism from many senior businessmen for years—people saying I was too young, too inexperienced, too arrogant, too timid … Hell, I'm sure "too short" was thrown in there at least once! But I had many great qualities that emerged as CEO, including a teachable spirit to counter my lack of experience, and a growing sense of introspection to counter my youthful overconfidence. Naked grew into a well-run, reasonably successful garment company with a growing brand and solid retail reach across North America.

We'd done well enough to attract some pretty big investors, and after I'd taken the company public I found myself visiting New York more and more to meet with major fashion industry players. Things were starting to get really big, at least to me, and I was starting to wonder if Naked was outgrowing me. I'd always been learning on the job, but this no longer felt like something I could just bumble through.

As I've said, I met some amazing people in New York, and there was one in particular who I felt shared my vision and my passion for Naked. She was the opportunity I'd been holding out for, an archetypal Big Apple success; a thriving nine figure underwear and sleepwear business, a TV show, and a rolodex that included just about anyone you needed to know in apparel. As the opportunity seemed nearer than ever before, I wondered if it was time to consider handing over the reins of Naked.

The restaurant was called Artisanal. As soon as I stepped through the door I knew that it was a place I could never afford to dine at myself—at least not yet! It was lively and bright, and the aromas wafting past were heavenly. The looks from the staff were cool as I stepped forward, but that quickly changed when I said Carole's name. I was shown efficiently to a private room at the back of the restaurant, and I'd barely sat down before a variety of exotic cheeses were presented. Sparkling water was served, followed by a series of daily recommendations which went completely over my head.

Carole arrived more or less on time. That all by itself impressed me, after having spent years being cancelled on or bumped by important people. It suggested respect on her part, and it made me optimistic about this meeting.

It amazed me how she managed to comport herself with such elegant casualness. There was nothing pretentious in her dress or demeanor, but at the same time she commanded attention. Her smile as she greeted me looked genuine, and even had a glimmer of excitement.

I only hoped that I wasn't grinning foolishly as I rose and warmly shook her hand.

"Hi, Carole. It's great to see you."

"It's great to see you too," she said as the waiter held out her chair for her. "How long are you in New York this time?"

"Just for two days, and I'm headed to the airport from here."

"The life of a young business mogul." Her eyes sparkled with humor.

I shrugged. "Aspiring mogul, maybe. I've got a long way to go yet, I think."

"But you'll make it."

She ordered us both some white wine, slipping easily into friendly conversation about travelling, families, and even the merits of a nice glass of vino. I forced myself to relax and just go with the flow. The wine helped—as expected from a restaurant like this it was truly excellent, and I had to pace myself to ensure my mind stayed sharp. This wasn't just a social call: I had an agenda.

She asked about Naked several times, but always in passing. Whenever I tried to stay on that topic she'd somehow manage to slide into another topic with such skill that I didn't even notice until it was too late. I couldn't steer the conversation back on my own. But she kept circling back obliquely as the delicious lunch progressed. It didn't feel like a test, and it certainly wasn't a pitch, but I honestly didn't know what it was.

She was friendly and fun, though, and the fact that she'd agreed to have a fourth meal with me at all must mean something. As coffee was poured—and a discreet glance at my watch told me that I needed to head soon for the airport—she opened the door for me.

"So what it is you want from me at Naked?" she asked.

I'd already asked her at previous meetings to invest in the company, but her question allowed me to be blunt.

"Carole," I said, leaning forward and forcing myself to meet her eyes, "I'd really like you to be the CEO of Naked. I know that you have everything that our company needs to really succeed. I'm just a business mogul-in-training: you're the real thing." I paused for just a moment. "How can we make that happen?"

Her expression barely shifted, but I knew I could see real interest in her eyes. She sipped at her coffee, then set the cup down softly in the saucer.

"Joel, your timing is perfect. I just came out of a non-compete clause from my last company … and I'm considering my options."

Her gentle demeanor was so disarming that I struggled to fully comprehend her words. Figuring out how to get Carole into Naked was going to take time—it was probably going to be more complicated than I could imagine, but she was exactly what we needed, and I just had a feeling that she would be the perfect fit.

She leaned back and sipped her coffee again. "You never know what the future holds, Joel."

My gut churned and my adrenaline starting pumping. I didn't like the sounds of that. I needed to know what the future held—at least this one time! I had to act. Looking around the table briefly I realized the pristine white tablecloth was lined with a large square piece of white paper, to make re-setting easier no doubt. An idea popped into my head.

"Okay," I said, pulling out a pen from my briefcase. "Let's make this official!"

Quickly, I cleared some space and wrote a contract right on the paper tablecloth, outlining that Carole would be our CEO and make Naked the next great underwear company in the world. I spoke out loud as I wrote so Carole could hear me. When it was done I signed it, carefully tore the section I'd written on clean off and handed it and my pen over to Carole.

"Please sign this," I said, grinning ear to ear. "You know we can do this."

She let out a small, friendly laugh, looked at me with a bemused expression and then signed the tablecloth.

Transitions

Don't be afraid of change. Embrace it.

Life comes with many transitions. We can go from the innocent and carefree days of our childhood to the confusing, yet hopefully still somewhat carefree, years of being a teenager. Then we experience the exhilaration of freedom in our 20s, when we're old enough to make good choices but we're still allowed to make bad ones! Then in our 30s things become a little more serious; some of us are still hanging onto our youth but the responsibilities and search for meaning that inevitably come make us into adults. There may still be lingering insecurities about who we are and our place in the world but by our 40s we should be past most of it which should set us up nicely for our 50s—or so I'm told.

One of my mentors once told me the journey through the decades for an entrepreneur is as follows: "Your 20s are for making mistakes, your 30s are for applying those mistakes, your 40s are for making money, your 50s are for spending some money and your 60s are when you give back and do estate planning."

Transitions, of course, are not just about age. We can go from being single to being in a relationship (and back again ...) or being child-free to having a minivan-worth of lovely little dependents. We can go from feeling 100% healthy to being ill or disabled. And, of course, we can go from being the chief of the company we founded to being subordinated or even jobless.

My mom always told me, "Seasons are for the soul." I've always thought about these "transitions" as seasons: sometimes it's dark and rainy, other times slow or dormant. Still other times it's chaotic like a storm, and others it's relaxing like those slow, sunny summer days. As each season passes, we grow (not just physically, but spiritually or professionally). Opportunities sprout where there were none before and yes, things pass away as well.

How we feel toward the seasons of our lives is much like how we feel toward the weather itself: the weather is what it is—viewing it positively or negatively is just the personal interpretation we impose upon it. We may have liked the freedom of our 20s a hell of a lot more than having to be an adult in our 30s, but that's not going to change how old we are, so we're better off accepting our new reality and looking for the good in it.

Each transition can serve a purpose in our own growth as human beings. And it's this growth—be it professional, personal, or spiritual—that breathes a sense of purpose into the experience.

As Naked continued to progress in what certainly felt like the right direction I put more and more energy into the company. But a lot had changed since the initial start-up days and there were a lot more people putting pressure on me to change this or change that. Alex and I had often disagreed on business decisions but we'd always at least been willing to listen to each other and talk our ideas through. But now Alex had left, and I was navigating huge changes in the company without his solid advice.

There were numerous strategic investment deals being offered to Naked. Some were immediate, others not so. Each had its pros and cons, and I'd already spent endless hours on banking calls and in deliberation over my options. The idea of bringing someone like Carole on board to help me make these decisions (or, who was I kidding, make them for me) was enticing. But was I really ready to hand control of my company to someone else?

I was torn. But one night, when the baby was down peacefully and Janna and I lay in a warm bath, I asked my wife what I should do.

Her answer, calm, caring as always, was: "Follow your heart, Joel. It already knows what to do."

So I did. I formally offered Carole the position as CEO of Naked. If the company was going to continue to grow and change, I had to change with it. We don't always like change. It can be difficult, even threatening, for some of us.

Radical change can be hard to deal with. It can feel like a direct threat to your survival. And if you don't do the personal growth work on yourself in your journey as an entrepreneur, you can have a hard time when you inevitably face it.

9

Letting Go

Joel. What are you going to do in New York?

Twelve months earlier, Carole had asked me that question. She'd asked it just a few weeks before we were supposed to finalize the deal to bring her on as our CEO and Chairperson. We'd raised nearly $7.5 million dollars and built out a team of industry executives from Armani, Ralph Lauren, Brooks Brothers and Calvin Klein.

She was asking me what role I'd play in the company when she became CEO and all the C-suite executives came on board.

It was, if you can believe it, a question I hadn't thought about. I guess I thought I'd just do everything I always did. I hadn't realized how that just didn't make sense, now that Carole was the chief executive and decision-maker of the company.

Eventually, after numerous discussions and at least a few sleepless nights contemplating my strengths and weaknesses (and self-worth as a whole), I learned that Carole and some of the key executives had decided to appoint me President of the company. This appointment came with a kind and encouraging note from Carole about opportunity in front of me, and that I had to learn and grow.

But something inside me had been rattled, opened-up, un-set by the process. I didn't know exactly what was bothering me or why, but I felt 'uncomfortable in my own skin'. And with no time to really think about it or talk with anyone, I was on a plane to New York, family in tow, jumping with both feet into a completely new life.

With Naked fully relocated to New York and me working with our new CEO and world-class executive management team, I was instantly star struck. Wanting to be respectful of the accomplishments of my new colleagues and partners, I often fell victim to feeling like an imposter in my own company: I felt like I no longer belonged.

I was grateful to have found a truly amazing person like Carole, well-situated in the industry, who was as determined and passionate about the business as I was. But after she took over the job as CEO, I had a much harder time with the transition than I expected, even though I thought I'd been mentally prepared to hand over the reins.

It wasn't giving up control that I struggled with the most, since Carole was so obviously wise, experienced, and she made smart decisions. What I struggled with was finding a new place for myself in the new Naked.

This is common for entrepreneurs, and if you continue working with your company in some capacity, you may feel the same at some point. Further, as I was no longer the ultimate decision-maker, I had to catch myself from feeling frustrated about how I might have done something differently. I came to the conclusion it was best to keep my focus where I could add the most value … which appeared to be raising money, keeping existing shareholders happy, and being the boots on the ground evangelist for the brand with our stores and their teams.

That was until the moment George, our new head of operations, said it was time to stop shipping our product to Canada.

To properly set the stage for my Midtown meltdown, it's important to add some context. You see, on top of already feeling like an imposter, I was feeling particularly self-loathing and shitty about myself. I'd just returned from Abbotsford where I'd personally notified my staff that our Abbotsford offices would be closing and that all of the Abbotsford staff—my wonderful team!—wouldn't be continuing on with the company. I'd clearly deluded myself with the idea that a cross-continental operation between New York and Abbotsford could work, and the harsh reality hadn't taken long to become clear. Still I was feeling physically sick over the decision, convinced that I hadn't fought hard enough for them.

I tried to console myself by searching for excuses and the ones I chose as my crutch were: *I had no choice. I couldn't risk the deal not closing. I couldn't risk that for the shareholders.* But we always have a choice. And although I learned through that process, not just how much I valued my team members but loved them, I lost a great deal of respect for myself.

Alright, back to the matter of my meltdown around our Canadian distribution shutdown.

Business is a tough proposition. I get it. Profits are king and I couldn't deny that since our warehousing had moved to New Jersey our Canadian business was no longer a profitable endeavor.

"We've done what we can," George said as we stood in the middle of the office hallway where everyone could see and hear us. "I've done my best to keep this alive, Joel. But I'm not going to report these numbers to the board. It won't be my ass on the line."

No question George had wanted to get rid of Canada sooner. I knew it was Carole who'd jumped in previously and vetoed the suggestion. But I wasn't ready to hear it.

"Those stores built this business, George. They didn't abandon me when I needed them. They represent the soul and the foundation of our company."

My voice cracked and I could feel my eyes watering. *Great, I thought, now I'm crying in front of a bunch of hardened New York executives.*

"Don't be myopic, Joel," George countered, with a touch of impatience. "California is bigger than Canada and we don't have to deal with an entirely different duty structure to ship."

"You wouldn't have had to if you hadn't shut down the Canadian warehouse and switched factories to begin with," I barked, standing as if I was going to get punched in the face.

"Because our manufacturer wouldn't split shipments from the factory to Canada and US," he shot back, gesturing angrily. "You know this, Joel."

"You just didn't try hard enough to get them to. Besides, we could have done that here and just done a duty drawback on goods instead of making our stores pay for that themselves."

Anger never solves anything, but I was angry.

Truth was, George was just trying to do his job as best he knew how. And to his credit he worked damn hard for Naked trying to do just that. The difference was that to George this was a job and nothing was personal. To me everything was personal. On a scale of 1 to 10 my emotional investment in Naked was 11. The fact that I was red-faced and misty-eyed in front of my team made it clear that my objectivity was compromised.

"This business was built in Canada," I said, trying to calm down. "And whether it's a smaller market than New Hampshire I don't care! Those who helped build this company shouldn't have to pay more."

George felt bad, I could see it on his face. Carole came out of her office and gave me a hug.

"We'll look at it all again," she said. "See if there is anything we can do." I guess deep down a mother is always a mother and in that moment I appreciated it.

But before long Canada was shut down and in the coming weeks and months I dealt with my first dose of hate mail. Sell out certain emails read. *Too big time for Canada, now?* said others. *I remember when Naked used to be made in Canada ... now it's all China-made garbage!*

In the history of entrepreneurs enduring public and private scrutiny, my trial was small ... But each email stung, because I agreed with them. The silver lining was that people had really cared about our product and I guess that counted for something.

Ultimately, I was arguing over spilt milk. The decision to stop shipping product to Canada made perfect business sense ... and Naked wasn't my business anymore. Of course, over the following months many more changes were made and I was struggling to see that these decisions were now outside my control.

Mentorship

Despite the story I just shared, ultimately that experience was full of important lessons. Lessons that, if you're like me and are fortunate enough to continue on with your company after new management comes on board, you need to take note of. Be open to all that you can learn and remember that the key is to just keep doing the work. Focus on your strengths. Listen to your gut and body ... how does it feel about what's happening? Keep sharing your ideas. Stay focused on your "why." Review your personal and professional goals and prepare for those tough moments. And above all, seek mentorship.

Seeking mentorship is important throughout every stage of your business, but it's particularly important in times of radical change. If you've found the right mentor, they've probably been in the exact same position you are today. The excuses you tell yourself about how *people just don't understand, or I don't know what to do*, will not work on the right mentor. They know and, more importantly, they're emotionally removed from the situation so they can give you a much-needed independent perspective. Even if a mentor agrees with your decision, it's just nice to get things off your chest without potential shareholder, director or employee backlash. Often, it's the mentor who will help you ask yourself the right questions ... especially when you're too stressed to see the answers you probably already know.

1. Am I still the right person for this job?

2. How do I focus on where I want to go?

3. What questions are coming up for me and what questions should I focus on?

4. Are there other options available to me to help make a better decision?

5. Am I no longer being true to my values and principles?

6. How am I feeling?

7. What do I need?

8. What's working?

9. What's not working?

10. What can I be thankful for?

11. What can I let go of?

12. Am I on path? (i.e. the path I want to be on.)

With all these things and more, a mentor can help you see where you need to improve or help you examine your conclusions objectively. Being able to see and identify those areas where we need to improve is one of the only ways we actually grow. In that way, a mentor can stimulate, or even super-charge, your personal and professional growth. The business landscape and the decisions you'll need to make are complex and we all need the energy, care, and clarity a mentor can provide to move through them. Even Steve Jobs had a mentor!

Know When to Exit

Knowing when to leave your start-up is the single hardest question a founder must ask himself or herself. Have you fallen out of love with the business you started? Is your "why" still there? Do you still have enough equity to feel the proper incentive to continue? Will your post-transition role make good use of your skill sets—does it matter if they don't? Will you be able to contribute meaningfully? Has the stress of the business and its wear and tear on your personal life made you resent what you do? Has the business reached a point where you genuinely believe someone else is better suited to lead?

Or, is the business successful and it's time to quit while you're ahead?

If you're thinking any of these thoughts, then take the appropriate time to really think about your decision. This may include time in nature away from the business, a reading vacation, or just focused meditation—whatever suits you best.

This is a decision for the mind and the heart. Fully think through all the possible consequences and, ultimately, follow your heart. It's a feeling that will drive "the right choice." You followed your heart into the business and you need to follow your heart out of it.

A mentor should also be able to help you assess whether your thinking is short-term or long-term. Do you have blind spots in your thinking patterns that may miss the opportunity cost attached to a decision?

What if you don't have to commit 100% to leaving? I'm the first to admit my undying love for the thrill of the "all or nothing" mentality—remember the example of Burning the Ships when starting your business in Chapter 2? Does it have to be a reverse scenario for leaving your business?

There's life-changing power in regular self-inquiry, but don't get caught up wallowing in the misery of too many choices or options or "what if" scenarios. You need to make sure you're looking for the signs and are willing to make decisions. There's a great story about this called the Drowning Man:

"A fellow was stuck on his rooftop in a flood. He was praying to God for help.

Soon a man in a rowboat came by and the fellow shouted to the man on the roof, 'Jump in, I can save you.'

The stranded fellow shouted back, 'No, it's okay, I'm praying to God and He is going to save me.'

So the rowboat went on.

Then a motorboat came by. The fellow in the motorboat shouted, 'Jump in, I can save you.'

To this the stranded man said, 'No thanks, I'm praying to God and He is going to save me. I have faith.'

So the motorboat went on.

Then a helicopter came by and the pilot shouted down, 'Grab this rope and I will lift you to safety.'

To this the stranded man again replied, 'No thanks, I'm praying to God and He is going to save me. I have faith.'

So the helicopter reluctantly flew away.

Soon the water rose above the rooftop and the man drowned. He went to Heaven. He finally got his chance to discuss this whole situation with God, at which point he exclaimed, 'I had faith in you, but you didn't save me, you let me drown. I don't understand why!'

To this God replied, 'I sent you a rowboat and a motorboat and a helicopter, what more did you expect?'" [6]
Once you recognize the signs or just "feel" it's time to leave, you'll

only cause a drain on your business if you stay too long. It's better to plan your exit and discuss with your partners and directors on how to best do that so it doesn't adversely affect the business or your shareholders.

They may be upset, but act with integrity. When you do what you believe to be the right thing, even if the results are not what was expected, your integrity remains intact; and your followers' confidence in you is not irreparably damaged, because they know you are a person of integrity.

Integrity is a principle that never fails and a principle that often goes without notice, upheld by only yourself. This doesn't mean you won't trip, stumble and fall a little. You're not perfect, but you act in accordance with your values and ensure that you're considering the good of everyone—not just yourself. Maybe shareholders will slander you; maybe the media will too. A mentor of mine always said one of his filters was, "Would I tell my children about the way I conducted myself and the choices I made in this moment?"

Sometimes, your departure may feel like a grand ceremony with swans and golden trumpets. Other times it will feel more like a slow crash and burn. But one way or another all things do come to an end. Assessing your personal and profession situation and then planning your exit integrally and strategically is the key to success here.

Trust the Process

You will always find a way forward. And often the most challenging path is the one you should be on.

Great things take time. Big returns don't come overnight. Yes, we live in a time where billion-dollar valuations are given to businesses in record time frames (bless you if that happens for you). That, however, isn't the norm and it's a dangerous mindset to adopt both personally and professionally. You set yourself up for continued

---

6 The Drowning Man. (n.d.). Truthbook. Retrieved from: https://truthbook.com/stories/funny-god/the-drowning-man

success by being patient, focused on your foundation, learning from failures, building happy teams with great culture, and enjoying yourself along the way.

The work of an entrepreneur is not about being rich or even happy. No, an entrepreneur is about being whole, proud of what you do and how you do it.

An entrepreneur's journey is intense, challenging, and filled with the unknown. It's through obstacles that we learn and grow.

As modern Stoic Ryan Holiday says, "The impediment to action advances action and what stands in the way becomes the way. The benefits are embedded inside the obstacles."

But from obstacles we learn how to deal with things again; you're not *getting over or through* something in your business or in your life. By experiencing the obstacle you're gaining tools and wisdom that make you feel different about things when you face it again.

In other words, you'll be ready: how to not fail at work, how to not enter bad relationships, how to not self-sabotage; how to get through financial struggles, or personality clashes at the office, or bad press— in time we learn from the obstacles and they become less and less obstacles … maybe they even become allies.

This teaches us that there's a certain something inside us—a power, if you will—that can endure and overcome the challenges our businesses and lives throw at us. We can keep moving forward, despite these challenges, even if we aren't 100% sure of the exact answers or path forward.

This also involves a certain surrendering to the process. Not resignation, where we throw our hands up in the air and say "well, what am I supposed to do now," but an *amor fati,* a love of fate, toward our path in entrepreneurship and life. As Joseph Campbell said, "We must be willing to let go of the life we planned so as to have the life that is waiting for us."

I often think of life and entrepreneurship as akin to water's journey from the mountains to its ultimate goal of reaching the ocean. Along the way it puts out different feelers, assessing different paths on its journey. It tries to avoid going up stream, for that's too hard, but ultimately it still has to break through rocks. Over time, with relentless effort, it forms canyons and paths where there were none before. Sometimes it rushes and rages, crashing over boulders, and other times it flows with ease. Still, it may reach an impasse, slowly rising and building power until it spills over the top and sides. Despite the obstacles it continues to find a way.

And then the river reaches its goal of joining the ocean—freedom—success—personal achievement—with the path behind clearly marking its long, arduous journey.

There it rests, for a moment, for a while, only to be evaporated back up into the sky and be snowed and rained right back down onto earth to begin yet another journey.

Is that not what we entrepreneurs do? Is that not what life is? Wouldn't you do it all over again too? If the answer yes, then you know you chose the right path.

Grieve Your Business

Stylish and charismatic as ever, NBA superstar Dwyane Wade sat to my right. In front of us, a crowd of bloggers, fashion influencers, and TV reporters lobbed questions at us.

The event was the launch of the Wade X Naked underwear line at Nordstrom in downtown Chicago. Our products lined the shelves and banners of Wade X Naked, or Mr. Wade himself in the products, lined the walls of the private room we'd built out in the middle of the menswear section of the floor. Most of the questions were directed at

Dwyane or his stylist, but occasionally one would be floated my way. "What makes Naked great?" "How did you start this company?" Stuff like that …

It should have been a triumphant moment, something I would have dreamed about when I first started Naked all those years ago. But my excitement wasn't what it should have been. Sitting here beside one my childhood heroes, talking about a product line we'd built together, was probably the single coolest moment of my entire life. Yet deep down, I knew my days at Naked were numbered.

A few months prior, following a presentation I'd given at a conference in California, a large Australian underwear company called Bendon Lingerie had an expressed interest in merging with Naked. After months of negotiation, independent fairness opinions, and board meetings, we'd agreed this merger was in the best interest of shareholders. At the time, Bendon had 4500 store partners around the world, they owned the licenses to brands like Heidi Klum, Stella McCartney and Fredericks of Hollywood, all brands far larger than Naked.

Although post-merger they intended to keep the New York office, their main operation would be in Sydney, Australia, and my time with the company was, in all likelihood, done. Yet again, radical change was coming.

Your business is like your baby. You've likely spent more of your awake time on your business than anything else in your life. If you've ever lost anything you loved, you know what it feels like to grieve. It's the same with the business: the role you used to have, the relationships you made that were specific to that business, all of it—gone.

Of course, some of those relationships can last a lifetime but you may be surprised just how quickly people move on to other things that capture their attention.

I know that may sound crazy, but remember that, as founder, your business is woven into your identity. Even if it's your choice to leave, you'll have to do the mental and emotional work associated with grieving and letting go to ensure that you can properly move on and prosper with other business ventures.

After the merger was complete, the NASDAQ bell was rung, and millions more dollars were raised into the company, my time at Naked had come to an end—but it did not end well.

Following the merger, over the course of a year, our combined companies lost hundreds of millions in shareholder value. Eventually, Bendon sold the Naked brand and shut down their entire US operations. So many shareholders had trusted us, trusted me, to deliver on their investment, but our stock was worth almost nothing. Although the company remained, so much value was lost.

The crushing feeling that followed these events felt like a slow death. Ten years of my life's work seemed to be undone in the span of months. Failure, guilt and remorse ached in my bones and shattered my self-confidence. I tried my best to give to my wife, my children, and my friends all of my love and presence, but thriving was hardly an option—all I was trying to do was survive.

Guilt haunted my days and nights and I'd wake up in cold sweats. People had lost money! I was also embarrassed that who I thought I was as a person was no more. Without Naked, and without Naked's success, I felt worthless.

For years I'd occasionally suffered from anxiety and depression, but nothing like this. My thoughts were clouded and negative, I experienced tiredness, shortness of breath, a hollow feeling in my chest, and a pronounced sense of negativity toward myself.

The more I tried to just "feel better" the more frustrated I became with everything. It was like snorkeling in shallow waters: the harder I kicked my flippers the more sand blocked my vision.

I'd view influencers and entrepreneurs on Instagram or YouTube and feel sick with envy. Heck, I even felt resentment toward some of my friends, whom I loved, who were achieving success. It was a terrible way to feel and a terrible way to live.

At the time, I viewed the loss of Naked as a regression of my personal and professional development.

But in the months that followed, quite the opposite happened. In many respects, leaving Naked put me on a better path. It forced me to face my demons (those negative stories I'd learned to tell myself) and to overcome my tendencies to be self-involved. Through adversity, I had the opportunity to learn and grow every day.

I realized that I had no choice but to mourn the business. I had to face my feelings of regret and my own beliefs around self-worth and why this experience affected me so deeply.

If this sort of thing happens to you, you're going to have to reveal your wounds and then metabolize them in some way in order to heal.

Recognizing, facing, and understanding each pain as it surfaces in the present moment may mean you have to relive the experience to some degree. Your ego won't want that to happen. It'll resist your efforts to be vulnerable, to forgive and let go because, each time you do—each time you work through a layer of pain—the ego loses a bit more control.

As one of my mentors reminded me, "It can take as long to wade out of the water as it did to wade in."

For me, the path of least resistance was to cast aside thoughts about Naked and my past experiences, and refuse to let them define me. But the more valuable path was instead to acknowledge them. I acknowledged their importance in shaping my character, my acumen, the lines on my face and the grey hairs on my head. They didn't define me, but they were certainly part of me.

It was about getting naked, in other words. Shattering those stories I'd come to believe were true about me was a disruptive process, but the parts of that process I've achieved thus far have been liberating.

Maybe it was true, that without Naked I was nothing. But only in the sense that the Naked journey shaped me into the person I am today! Sure, without it there would have been other experiences that shaped me differently—but this is my experience, and I need to always honor that!

On my last day in the New York office I walked in quietly and, before being noticed, I snuck into our showroom. Rows and rows of product lined the shelves, ready for the next buyer meetings. Most were Carole's designs but still there, in the midst of it, was that one smooth, waistband-less black pair of underwear with a tiny "Naked" logo on the side. I picked it up and walked over to the window overlooking the bustling, yellow cab filled, Madison Avenue. I couldn't help but let the nostalgia pulse through me—who'd have thought?

After replacing the sample I headed down the hallway to Carole's office. It was a small room, which I respected. Despite all her personal and professional success here she was, working away in a tiny cubical-sized office.

This wasn't exactly the goodbye Carole or I would have wanted. The current state of affairs with the Bendon purchase wasn't what we'd hoped when we signed that tablecloth in what seemed an age ago.

She had her usual warm, stoic air about her. I knew she was a seasoned professional, so maybe this sort of merger and change was just business as usual? Maybe ... but looking into her sad eyes I didn't think so. She was a pro, but she always cared deeply for whatever she got involved in. Even so, her poise was unshakable. I was trying to be just as professional, but I was overwhelmed with the combination of joy, fear, sorrow, excitement, and shame of everything that had happened combined with the uncertainty of what might come next.

I handed Carole a book and hand-written card. Of course there was likely nothing in that book that she didn't already know. It was a nothing more than peace offering. An old habit. An "I'm not exactly sure what to say ... so here's a small gift."

She smiled. She rose from her desk, came around and hugged me. And said, "You'll be fine, Joel."

And that was that. I grabbed a taxi, headed to Penn Station and then took a train to airport. My family was already back at home in Vancouver.

Naked, Alex, Abbotsford, the Dragons, New York, Carole, Dwyane, the good, the bad, the terrible, all of it. It had all been a gift—a gift that would give me the tools to ensure Carole's parting words could become true.

I didn't know what the future held. Like any entrepreneur I usually had endless ideas floating around in my head but in that moment they were nowhere to be found. It wasn't a moment to look forward but instead back. Back to apartment kitchens that weren't kitchens at all but workshops of discovery and creation. Back to the eyes of investors who were truly angels—not investing money in a business but breathing life into a dream. Back to a cold warehouse without a sign that so boldly held the hopes and dreams of young aspiring people. And back to loyal friends and team members—especially one, one who stood as strong as he knew how beside me, looked beyond failures and mistakes, so many mistakes, eager to see if we could make it happen.

Standing there, as all the thoughts danced from my head to my heart I could have sworn, even if it was just in my bones and in my blood, my foot was gently tapping to the beat of Michael Jackson.

And then I thought of my family. And I couldn't wait to get home.

Appendix

This appendix is filled with resources and recommendations from myself and a few fellow entrepreneurs.

<u>Book Resources</u>

Business, Start Up, Management, and Marketing Books:

All Marketers Are Liars by Seth Godin
Blue Ocean Strategy by W. Chan Kim & Renée A. Mauborgne
Built to Last: Successful Habits of Visionary Companies by Jim Collins and Jerry I. Porras
Crossing the Chasm: Marketing and Selling Disruptive Products to Mainstream Customers by Geoffrey A. Moore
Fooled by Randomness: The Hidden Role of Chance in Life and in the Markets by Nassim Nicholas Taleb
Getting to Yes: Negotiating Agreement Without Giving In by Roger Fisher & William Ury
Good to Great: Why Some Companies Make the Leap ... And Others Don't by Jim Collins
High Output Management by Andrew S. Grove
Made to Stick: Why Some Ideas Survive and Others Die by Chip Heath & Dan Heath
The Lean Startup by Eric Ries
Poor Charlie's Almanack: The Wit and Wisdom of Charles T. Munger by Peter D. Kaufman
Purple Cow: Transform Your Business by Being Remarkable by Seth Godin
The Effective Executive: The Definitive Guide to Getting the Right Things Done by Peter F. Drucker

The One-Minute Manager by Kenneth Blanchard & Spencer
Johnson
Who Moved my Cheese? An A-Mazing Way to Deal with Change
in Your Work and in Your Life by Spencer Johnson

Lifestyle, Design & Principles

Atomic Habits: An Easy & Proven Way to Build Good Habits &
Break Bad Ones by James Clear
Essentialism: The Disciplined Pursuit of Less by Greg McKeown
Extreme Ownership by Jocko Willink & Leif Babin
Getting Things Done: The Art of Stress-Free Productivity by David
Allen
The 4-Hour Workweek by Tim Ferriss
Thrive: The Third Metric to Redefining Success and Creating a Life
of Well-Being, Wisdom, and Wonder by Arianna Huffington
Tribe of Mentors by Tim Ferriss

Mindset

Abundance: The Future is Better Than You Think by Peter
Diamandis & Steven Kotler
As a Man Thinketh by James Allen
Bold: How to Go Big, Create Wealth and Impact the World by Peter
Diamandis & Steven Kotler
The Magic of Thinking Big by David J. Schwartz
The Obstacle Is the Way by Ryan Holiday
The Science of Getting Rich by Wallace D. Wattles
Wherever You Go, There You Are by Jon Kabat-Zinn
You are a Badass: How to Stop Doubting Your Greatness and Start
Living an Awesome Life by Jen Sincero
You Are Awesome: How to Navigate Change, Wrestle with Failure,
and Live an Intentional Life by Neil Pasricha

Business Autobiography

Delivering Happiness by Tony Hsieh
Getting There: A Book of Mentors by Gillian Zoe Segal
How to Get Rich by Felix Dennis
Principles: Life and Work by Ray Dalio
The Fish That Ate The Whale: The Life and Times of America's
        Banana King by Rich Cohen
The Hard Thing About Hard Things by Ben Horowitz
Setting the Table: The Transforming Power of Hospitality in
        Business by Danny Meyer
Shoe Dog: A Memoir By the Creator of Nike by Phil Knight

Online Resources

Start Up Stash (the world's largest directory of tools and resources
for startups and entrepreneurs)

https://startupstash.com

Crowdsourcing Sales & Product Testing

Causes (for non-profits)
www.causes.com

Go Fund Me (for personal projects)
www.gofundme.com

Indiegogo
www.indiegogo.com

Kickstarter
www.kickstarter.com

Patreon (for creators)
www.patreon.com

Crowdsourcing Equity

Angel List
www.angel.co

Circle Up
www.circleup.com

Crowd Funder
www.crowdfunder.com

Front Fundr (Canadian)
www.frontfundr.com

Fundable
www.fundable.com

WeFunder
www.wefunder.com

Angel Investors

Crunchbase
www.crunchbase.com

Gust
www.gust.com

Keiretsu Capital
www.keiretsucapital.com

LinkedIn
www.linkedin.com

NACO: National Angel Capital Organization (Canada)
www.nacocanada.com

Start-Up Accelerators

Founder Institute
https://fi.co

Techstars
www.techstars.com

Women's Start Up Lab
www.womenstartuplab.com

Y Combinator
www.ycombinator.com

100 Top Accelerators Around the World
https://about.crunchbase.com/blog/100-startup-accelerators-around-the-world/

Ensure to look at your local City, State, or Province for Angel Investor Networks or Start-Up Accelerators

Task, Project Management, and Internal Communication

Asana
www.asana.com

Basecamp
www.basecamp.com

Mondays
www.mondays.com

Slack
www.slack.com

Trello
www.trello.com

Cloud Storage

Box.com
www.box.com

Dropbox
www.dropbox.com

Google Drive & Google Workspace (a comprehensive and easy-to-use platform for email, storage, and calendar management)
workspace.google.com

Freelancers (Graphic, Design, Web, Marketing, and More)

Fivverr
www.fiverr.com

Up Work
www.upwork.com

99 Designs
www.99designs.com

Email Marketing & Social Media

Hootsuite
www.hootsuite.com

Kylavio
www.kylavio.com

Later
www.later.com

Mailchimp
www.mailchimp.com

Accounting

Freshbooks
www.freshbooks.com

Websites

Shopify (ecommerce)
www.shopify.com

Squarespace
www.squarespace.com

WIX
www.wix.com

Wordpress
www.wordpress.com

URL Registration

Go Daddy
www.godaddy.com

Proxy Solicitation

Laurel Hill
www.laurelhill.com

Morrow Sodali
www.morrowsodali.com

Survey Tools

Survey Monkey
https://www.surveymonkey.com/

Investor Relations (for public companies)

CMA - Captial Markets Access Group - Investor Relations
www.capitalmarketaccess.com/cma-team

ICR - Strategy and Advisory
https://icrinc.com

MZ Group North America - Investor Relations
www.mzgroup.us

Other Tools

Boomerang (for Gmail)
www.boomeranggmail.com

Calendy
https://calendly.com

Free Image
www.Unsplash.com

A Few Resources My Partners Recommend

From Karyna McLaren:

1. Facebook Groups – look for niche FB Groups in your industry/region. These can be a great way to network and find clients. When I first started freelancing, I found almost all my clients in these

groups.

2. Futurpreneur (for Canadian entrepreneurs)

3. Harvard Business Review – just a great publication to subscribe to. Lots to learn through case studies.

4. Look for your local entrepreneur support organizations; there will likely be at least one, if not a few! They tend to offer free workshops/seminars, and you may get access to mentors, resources, etc. For example, we have the RIC Centre here in Toronto that helps Ontario start-ups!

5. Skillshare – a great way to learn new skills + fill in the blanks.

6. Shopify – my favorite e-commerce platform: easy to use with a tiered approach. Anyone can set up a website super quickly and affordably.

7. Spotify – a great playlist is a "must" to really hunker down and focus. Some of my favorites include <u>Good Vibes</u> (when I'm wanting something more pumped up), <u>Acoustic Cafe International</u> (when I want something more global/unique), <u>Provence Work Playlist</u> (when I REALLY need to focus).

8. StartUp Fest (for Canadian entrepreneurs)

9. Upwork – an awesome way to find help with a variety of task and topics; the quality here tends to be way better than Fiverr.

10. Wave – my favorite accounting software for freelancers. Allows you to manage everything in one place as well as invoicing.

From Faez Rawas:

1. App Sumo – daily deals on SaaS.

2. Blogs
- www.nateliason.com
- www.indiehackers.com

3. Built With – for checking out what technologies your favorite websites are using.

4. Facebook Ad Library – to see what your competition is targeting with ads.

5. Google Trends – for spotting trends.

6. Hunter – Google Chrome extension that finds you emails when visiting a website

7. Public Library – so much free knowledge!

8. Reddit – r/entrepreneur

9. Twitter
- @naval
- @paulg
- @julian

And One More, from My Long-Time Partner Alex McAulay

1. Business Model Canvas – a great tool to help you understand a business model in a straightforward, structured way: www.businessmodelsinc.com/about-bmi/tools/business-model-canvas

About The Author

An entrepreneur among other things, Joel Primus is the founder and creative visionary behind Naked Underwear. He helped raise over $17 million, establishing retail distribution at Holt Renfrew, Nordstrom, Hudson's Bay, and Bloomingdales. Naked completed a merger with Australian-based industry powerhouse, Bendon Lingerie, exiting in 2018. Recently, Joel co-founded Kosan, a travel clothing company which launched one of the most successful Kickstarter apparel products of all time—reaching nearly $1 million in sales in 30 days. He was one of the inaugural BC Business top 30 under 30 Entrepreneurs and is also an author and award winning documentary filmmaker.

Once an elite long distance runner, he now enjoys daily training, meditation, and time with his family on their farm outside Vancouver.

Other Work By
Joel Primus

I am deeply passionate about dedicating my time to helping executives and entrepreneurs to cultivate balance, inner strength, and wellbeing, as part of their path to personal and professional success.

You'll see how the different areas of your life—money, family, intimacy, and emotional well-being—can be handled all in the same coaching session ... and how a coach can utilize the body to create incredible healing.

As an individual experience, it does not matter to me whether you're a C-suite executive, a successful entrepreneur, a dreamer ready to start your first business, or just a lover of life. If you're courageous, committed and seeking the support needed to break through to a higher level, then I'm game. And if you've found your way here, I have no doubt you are!

21-Day Online Personal Transformation Course

- This online program is for individuals who are self-motivated and desire the tools to go beyond their current achievements and reach the next level.
- In this immersive course experience, we'll uncover the core of your current challenges, empower you to break through to a new way of thinking, and re-shape your habits as you design and live the life you truly seek.
- By signing up for this course, you will unlock powerful content that you can utilize and practice—forever.

Getting Naked – Online Start-Up Course for Entrepreneurs

- Coming soon!

Ongoing Professional & Personal Life Coaching & Start-Up Consultation

Visit www.joelprimus.com or contact hello@joelprimus.com to learn about all courses and consultation.

Manufactured by Amazon.ca
Bolton, ON

33175921R00143